PICTORIAL ARCHIVE OF
EARLY ILLUSTRATIONS
AND VIEWS OF
AMERICAN
ARCHITECTURE

PICTORIAL ARCHIVE OF
EARLY ILLUSTRATIONS
AND VIEWS OF
AMERICAN
ARCHITECTURE

Edmund V. Gillon Jr.

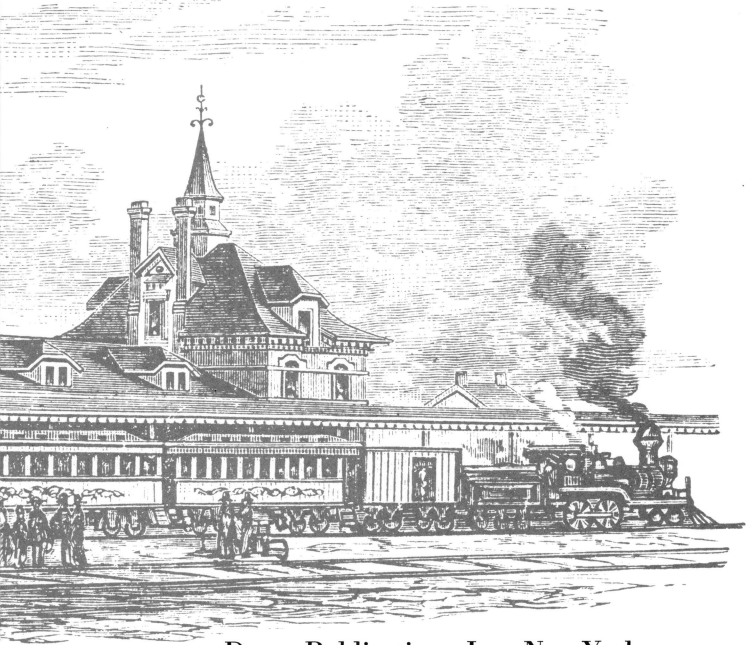

Dover Publications, Inc., New York

Published in Canada by General Publishing Company, Ltd., 30
Lesmill Road, Don Mills, Toronto, Ontario.
Published in the United Kingdom by Constable and Company,
Ltd.

Pictorial Archive of Early Illustrations and Views of American Architecture is
a new work, first published by Dover Publications, Inc., in 1971. The
sources of all the illustrations are indicated in the captions and the
Bibliography.

DOVER *Pictorial Archive* SERIES

International Standard Book Number: 0-486-22750-2
Library of Congress Catalog Card Number: 71-152420

Manufactured in the United States of America
Dover Publications, Inc.
31 East 2nd Street
Mineola, N.Y. 11501

Introduction

Nineteenth-century America was proud of its buildings and pleased to portray them in all graphic media. Home owners considered their dwellings as extensions of their personality and commissioned "portraits" of their property as well as of themselves. Civic pride inspired numerous publications depicting important or beloved local edifices. Lively illustrated periodicals kept abreast of new construction in major cities. Leading architects published handsome albums and catalogues of designs for residences and other buildings.

The many oil renderings of farms and estates by "primitive" painters like Edward Hicks and professionals like the Mounts are well known. The present volume is intended as an introduction to the wealth of architectural views published throughout the century in the various reproductive media in use before the age of photographic illustrations: wood engravings, steel engravings, electrotypes and photomechanical reproductions of pen drawings.

Included here are 742 pictures of buildings and views from printed sources, many now exceedingly rare, dating between 1839 and the early twentieth century. The buildings themselves range from circa 1615 to the late nineteenth century. They are (or were) located in 249 cities in 27 states and the District of Columbia. All major American architectural periods and styles are included: Colonial, Federal, Greek Revival, etc., with an especially heavy representation of Gothic Revival and the Victorian "eclectic."

The illustrations are generally arranged by categories (in approximate chronological order within the categories), as follows: streets, squares and town views (1–22); houses of worship (23–109); homes—cottages, town houses, mansions, villas, farm buildings (110–313); schools, colleges and academies (314–388); government edifices—city halls, state houses, post offices, prisons, police stations, courthouses (389–473); shops and businesses, commercial blocks and department stores (474–549); theaters and other places of entertainment (550–572); railroad stations (573–585); banks (586–598); institutions and hospitals (599–620); libraries, museums, exhibition and lodge buildings (621–637); taverns and hotels (638–682); mills and factories (683–716); firehouses, monuments, lighthouses, windmills and miscellaneous (717–742).

A fair number of famous buildings are depicted—some of them still standing (for example, Faneuil Hall, Cooper Union, Ford's Theatre, Independence Hall), some demolished (for example, the Hippodrome and many old buildings on Ivy League campuses). There are celebrated birthplaces (Monroe, Jackson, Daniel Webster) and residences (William Penn, John Hancock). There are works by such outstanding architects as Ammi Young, Peter Harrison and Charles Bulfinch, including a number of important structures no longer extant.

But this book has by no means been conceived as a scholarly record of high points in architecture. Instead, it offers a wide sampling of the everyday American scene as it appeared to nineteenth-century eyes. Buildings and views have been included not for their excellence or reputation, but for their representativeness and their direct depiction of the life of the times. These are not cold architectural drawings, but, for the most part, spirited renderings which place the buildings in their surroundings, along with the neighboring structures, on populous streets showing contemporary people at work and play. A particularly broad spectrum of mercantile and manufacturing activities is included; in the section devoted to stores, not only façades are shown, but also interiors and details of window displays. Among the great variety of structures we find Newport villas, barns and piggeries, an eighteenth-century coffee house, a pre-Civil War slave cabin, a synagogue modeled on the Alhambra, and pavilions from the 1876 Philadelphia Centennial. Freshness and immediacy enliven the accuracy and trustworthiness of the draftsmanship.

The captions to the illustrations include the following information (when available), in the following order: the name of the building; then, in parentheses, the year it was built, its architect, and information on alterations, demolition, etc.; then, the street it is (or was) located on, the city, and the date *of the picture*; finally, in square brackets, the number (in the Bibliography) of the printed source from which the picture was reproduced. For example:

Christ Church (built 1744 after a design by James Gibbs: James Porteus, architect; steeple added 1754: Harrison and Smith, architects), Second St., Philadelphia, Penn., c. 1853. [15]

Less concisely: Christ Church was built by James Porteus in 1744 after a design by James Gibbs; Harrison and Smith built the steeple that was added ten years later; the church is located on Second Street in Philadelphia; the picture of the church in the book was done about 1853; the source of the picture is item 15 in the Bibliography that appears on pages 287–288 of this book: *Gleason's Pictorial Drawing-room Companion*, etc.

The present volume also contains an Index of states, and cities within states, in which the buildings and views illustrated are located.

I hope that the reader will experience some of the surprise, respect and pleasure I felt upon discovering and rediscovering the extent and quality of this material bequeathed to us by the unsung graphic artists of the nineteenth century.

E. V. G.

Contents

PICTORIAL ARCHIVE OF
EARLY ILLUSTRATIONS
AND VIEWS OF
AMERICAN
ARCHITECTURE

1. Main St., Zanesville, Ohio, c. 1847. [22]

2. Old State House (built 1711: Robert Twelves, possible architect), State St., Boston, Mass., c. 1848. [38]

3. Dayton, Ohio, c. 1847. [22]

5. Fulton and Fronts Sts., Brooklyn, N.Y., c. 1816 [34]

4. *Washington, Ohio, c. 1847.* [22]

6. State St., Albany, N.Y., c. 1848. [38]

7. High St., Columbus, Ohio, c. 1847. [22]

8. Faneuil Hall (built 1742: John Smibert, architect; enlarged and rebuilt 1805: Charles Bulfinch, architect), Boston, Mass., c. 1848. [38]

9. Market St., Steubenville, Ohio, c. 1847. [22]

10. The Five Points, Junction of Baxter, Worth and Park Sts., New York, N. Y., c. 1829. [11]

11. Webb's Congress Hall, 142 Broadway, New York, N.Y.

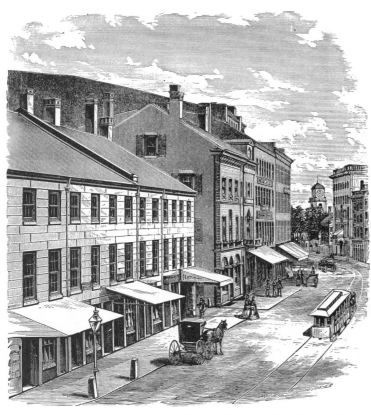

13. Doyers St., known locally as Shinbone Alley, New York, N.Y., 1891. [7]

12. Middle St., Portland, Maine, before the great fire of 1866. [14]

14. Market Square, Providence, R.I., c. 1844. [16]

15. Pottsville, Penn., c. 1843. [12]

16. Public square in Chambersburg, Penn., c. 1843. [12]

17. *Court House Square (Solomon Willard, architect), Dedham, Mass., c. 1835. [3]*

18. *Central part of Washington, Penn., c. 1843. [12]*

19. *Main St., Pawtucket, R.I., c. 1886.* [16]

20. *Exchange Place and the Union Depot, Providence, R.I., c. 1886.* [16]

21. Broad St., Westerly, R.I., c. 1886. [16]

22. Market Square and the Union Railroad Depot, Providence, R.I., c. 1886. [16]

24. *The first meeting house in West Springfield, Mass. (built 1702).* [18]

23. *First Congregational Church, "The Old Tunnel" (built 1682; remodeled 1827), the Common, Lynn, Mass.* [21]

26. *The first church in Cincinnati, Ohio (built 1792), c. 1847* [22]

25. *Christ Church, also known as Old North Church (built 1723: possibly from a design by Christopher Wren), Salem St., Boston, Mass., c. 1817.* [41]

27. *Old Trinity Church (built 1735; destroyed 1832), Summer and Hawley Sts., Boston, Mass., c. 1830.* [41]

28. *Congregational Church (built 1680), Hingham, Mass., c. 1874.* [31]

29. *Congregational Church (built 1680), Hingham, Mass.,* c. *1839.* [3]

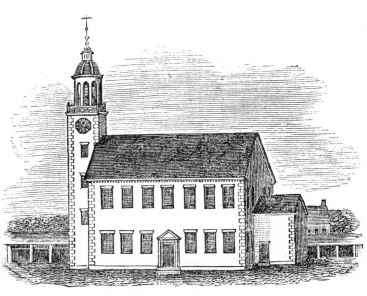

30. *First Congregational Church (built 1794), Brookfield, Mass.,* c. *1835.* [3]

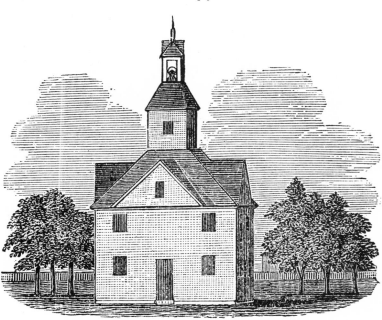

31. *The first church in West Springfield, Mass. (built 1702: John Allys, architect).* [3]

32. *Friends' Meeting House (built 1690), Haddonfield, N.J.,* c. *1842.* [2]

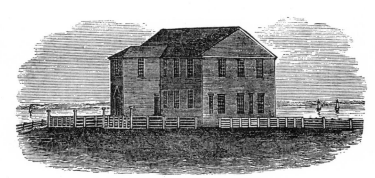

33. *Church, Truro, Mass.,* c. *1839.* [3]

34. *Old Town House, Benefit and College Sts., Providence, R.I.* [16]

35. *Lutheran church (erected 1743), Trappe, Penn.,* c. *1843.* [12]

36. *First Baptist Church (erected 1774; Joseph Brown, architect), N. Main St., Providence, R.I., c. 1886. [16]*

37. *Trinity Church (erected 1726; Richard Munday, architect), Spring and Church Sts., Newport, R.I., c. 1886. [16]*

38. *The Old Ballou Meeting House (built c. 1740), Cumberland, R.I. c. 1886. [16]*

39. Old Meeting House (built 1713; demolished c. 1848), Glouces-
ter, Mass., c. 1848. [35]

40. John St. Methodist Church (built 1768; demolished 1817),
44 John St., New York, N.Y. [40]

41. Federal St. Church (erected 1744; demolished c. 1807), Berry
and Federal Sts., Boston, Mass. [41]

42. The Old Quaker Meeting House (built 1704), Lincoln, R.I.,
c. 1886. [16]

43. *St. George's Chapel (erected 1752), Beekman St., New York, N.Y.*

44. Christ Church, also known as Old North Church (built 1723: possibly from a design by Christopher Wren), Salem St., Boston, Mass., c. 1889. [25]

45. The Old South (built 1729: Robert Twelves, architect), Washington and Milk Sts., Boston, Mass., c. 1889. [25]

46. First Parish Church (built 1825), Portland, Maine, c. 1876. [14]

47. Second Church (dedicated 1806), Washington St., Dorchester, Mass., c. 1889. [25]

48. King's Chapel (erected 1754: Peter Harrison, architect; colonnade by Charles Bulfinch), Tremont St., Boston, Mass., c. 1889. [25]

49. Christ Church (built 1744 after a design by James Gibbs: James Porteus, architect; steeple added 1754: Harrison & Smith, architects), Second St., Philadelphia, Penn., c. 1853. [15]

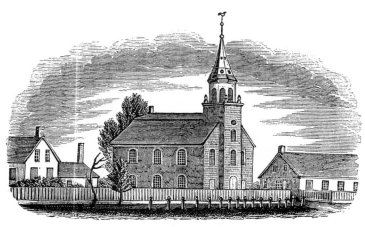

50. Reformed Dutch Church (built 1773; demolished 1841), Bergen, N.J., c. 1840. [2]

52. Christ Church, Second St., Philadelphia, Penn., c. 1853. [12]

51. Methodist Church, Englishtown, N.J., c. 1840. [2]

54. Presbyterian Church and Academy, Cranberry, N. J., c. 1868. [2]

53. "Old North" Congregational Church, Marblehead, Mass., c. 1875. [13]

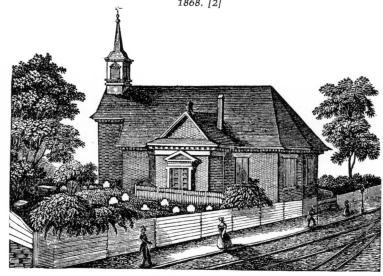

55. Old Swedes' Church (built 1700), Swanson St., Philadelphia, Penn., c. 1843. [12]

56. *St. George's Chapel (erected 1752), Beekman St., New York,*
N.Y.

Engraved by JAMES EDDY Wall St N.Y. from a drawing by A.J.DAVIS.

57. *St. Paul's Chapel (erected 1766: Thomas McBean, architect; tower added 1796: James C.*
Lawrence, architect), Broadway and Fulton Sts., New York, N.Y.

58. John St. Methodist Church (built 1841), 44 John St., New York, N.Y., c. 1881. [40]

59. Franklin St. Cathedral (erected 1803; demolished 1860), Boston, Mass., c. 1850. [41]

60. Mormon Temple (built 1835), Kirtland, Ohio. c. 1847. [22]

61. Park St. Church (erected 1810: Peter Banner, architect), Tremont St., Boston, Mass., c. 1889. [25]

62. Charles St. Church, Boston, Mass., c. 1853. [15]

64. *Presbyterian Church (erected 1796), Bloomfield, N.J., c. 1840.*
[2]

63. *Congregational Church, Sutton, Mass., c.
1878. [6]*

65. *Baptist Church (built 1829), Sutton, Mass.,
c. 1878. [6]*

66. *New South Church (built 1814: Charles Bulfinch, architect;
demolished 1868), Bedford and Summer Sts., Boston, Mass., c.
1835. [41]*

67. Welsh Church (erected 1717), Radnor, Penn., c. 1843. [12]

68. Church of Our Lady, Cold Spring, N.Y., c. 1848. [38]

69. Hollis St. Church (built 1788: Charles Bulfinch, architect; demolished 1810), Boston, Mass., c. 1793. [41]

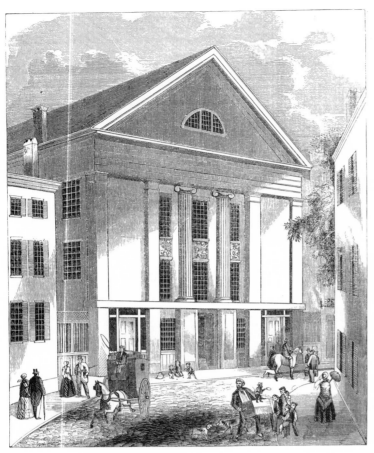

71. Mariners' Church, Portland, Maine, c. 1839. [29]

70. Fifth Universalist Church, Warren St., Boston, Mass., c. 1853. [15]

72. Baptist Church (built 1804), South Sutton, Mass., c. 1878. [6]

73. St. Peter's Cathedral (consecrated 1844: Henry Walters, probable architect), Plum St., Cincinnati, Ohio, c. 1848. [38]

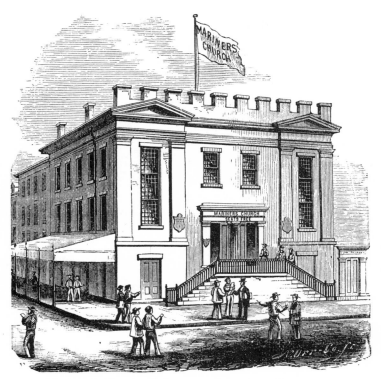

74. Mariners' Church, Catherine and Madison Sts., New York, N.Y., c. 1869. [39]

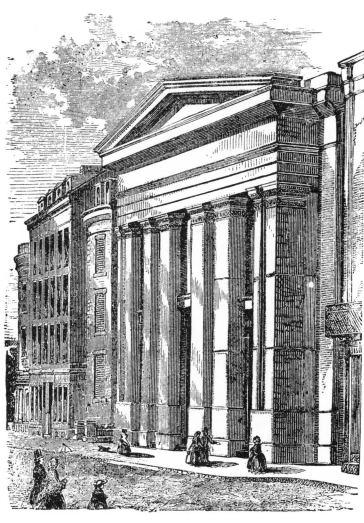

75. Mount Vernon Church (dedicated 1844), Ashburton Pl., Boston, Mass., c. 1889. [25]

76. First Baptist Church, Springfield, Mass.

77. The "First Church" (built 1837; burned 1870), Vine and S. Common Sts., Lynn, Mass. [21]

78. Broad St. Methodist Church, Richmond, Va., c. 1881. [40]

79. St. Peter's Cathedral (consecrated 1844: Henry Walters, probable architect), Plum St., Cincinnati, Ohio, c. 1848. [24]

80. East Baptist Church, Union St., Lynn, Mass., c. 1886. [21]

81. Winthrop Church, Holbrook, Mass., c. 1874. [31]

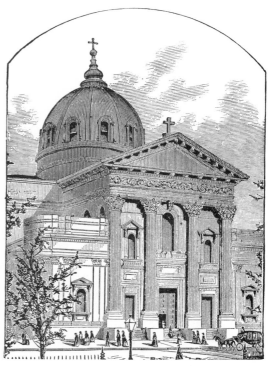

82. Cathedral of St. Peter and St. Paul (built 1864: Napoleon LeBrun and John Notman, architects), Eighteenth St., Philadelphia, Penn., c. 1876. [26]

CHURCHES 29

83. Congregational Church (erected 1868), Broadway and Walcott Sts., Pawtucket, R.I., c. 1886. [16]

84. Universalist Church, High St., Pawtucket, R.I., c. 1886. [16]

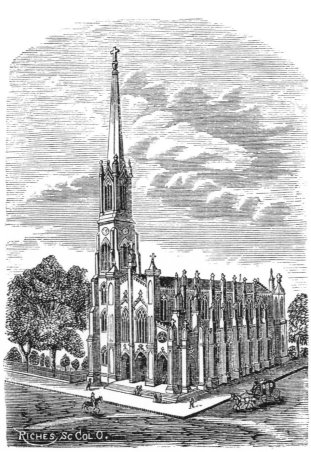

85. St. Joseph's Cathedral (work in progress 1873), Broad and Fifth Sts., Columbus, Ohio. [42]

86. Chestnut St. Methodist Episcopal Church (erected 1822), Chestnut and Clifford Sts., Providence, R.I., c. 1886. [16]

*87. St. John's Episcopal Church (erected 1810), North Main St.,
Providence, R.I., c. 1886. [16]*

*88. St. Patrick's Cathedral (built 1815: Joseph Mangin, architect;
rebuilt after fire 1868: Henry Englebert, architect), Mott and
Prince Sts., New York, N.Y., c. 1869. [39]*

89. Chapel, Mount Auburn Cemetery, Cambridge, Mass., c. 1849.
[35]

90. St. Thomas' Church (erected 1824; destroyed by fire, 1851), Broadway and Houston Sts.,
New York, N. Y., c. 1829.

91. St. Paul's Church, Albany, N.Y., c. 1848 [38]

92. St. Paul's Church, Troy, N.Y., c. 1848. [38]

93. Church, Gardiner, Maine, c. 1838. [29]

94. Howard St. Methodist Church, San Francisco, Calif., c. 1881. [40]

95. *St. Paul's Church, Worcester, Mass., c. 1874.* [31]

96. *The Cathedral of the Holy Cross (dedicated 1875), Washington St., Boston, Mass., c. 1889.* [25]

97. Union Methodist Church, St. Louis, Mo., c. 1881. [40]

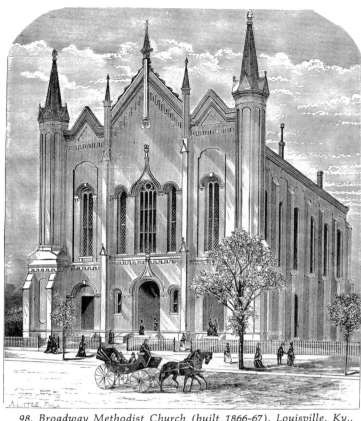

98. Broadway Methodist Church (built 1866-67), Louisville, Ky.,
c. 1881. [40]

99. First Methodist Church (built 1868), Muscatine, Iowa, c. 1881.
[40]

100. First Methodist Church (built 1870), Minneapolis, Minn.,
c. 1881. [40]

101. First Methodist Church (built 1848; rebuilt 1876), Atlanta,
Ga., c. 1881. [40]

102. K.K. Benai Jeshurun Hebrew Synagogue (dedicated 1866; designed after the Alhambra), Plum St., Cincinnati, Ohio, c. 1876. [24]

103. Second Universalist Church (erected 1872), Columbus Ave., Boston, Mass., c. 1889. [25]

104. Dudley St. Baptist Church (opened 1853), Boston, Mass., c. 1889. [25]

105. First Congregational Church (dedicated 1857: J. Moser, architect), Broad St., Columbus, Ohio, c. 1873. [42]

106. Lawrence St. Methodist Church (built 1864), Denver, Colo., c. 1881. [40]

107. St. John's Methodist Episcopal Church (cornerstone laid 1871), Longworth and Park Sts., Cincinnati, Ohio, c. 1876. [24]

108. The Old South Church (erected c. 1872), Boston, Mass., c. 1889. [25]

109. Arch St. Methodist Church (built 1873), Arch and Broad Sts., Philadelphia, Penn., c. 1876. [26]

110. Old Pynchon Mansion (built 1662; destroyed 1831), Main St., Springfield, Mass., c. 1784. [3]

111. Leonard House (erected c. 1670), Raynham, Mass., c. 1839. [3]

112. Old Pynchon Mansion (built 1662; destroyed 1831), Main St., Springfield, Mass. [18]

113. Julien's Restorator Inn (built 1760; demolished 1824), Milk and Congress Sts., Boston, Mass. [41]

114. Carpenter's Mansion, Chestnut St., Philadelphia, Penn.

115. *Old Garrison House (built c. 1615), York, Maine, c. 1893. [9]*

116. *Weaver's House (erected c. 1670), Medfield, Mass., c. 1839.*
[3]

117. *Captain Sheldon's House (erected prior to 1700), Deerfield,*
Mass., c. 1839. [3]

118. *Old Coddington House, Newport, R.I., c.*
1886. [16]

119. *Major Thomas Fenner's House (erected 1667), Cranston, R.I., c. 1886. [16]*

120. Slate-Roof House, residence of William Penn (built c. 1690: James Porteus, architect; demolished 1867), Third St., Philadelphia, Penn., c. 1853. [15]

121. Hasbrouch House, Newburg, N.Y., c. 1893. [9]

122. Vechte-Cortelyou House (built 1699), Third St., Brooklyn, N.Y., c. 1853. [15]

123. Cottage of a German-Swiss emigrant, Columbiana County, Ohio, c. 1847. [22]

124. Davenport House (built 1767), South Sutton, Mass., c. 1878. [6]

125. Shattuck House, Salem, Mass., c. 1875. [13]

126. Watson House, Clark's Island, Mass., c. 1875. [13]

127. Vernon House, Clark and Mary Sts., Newport, R. I., c. 1875. [13]

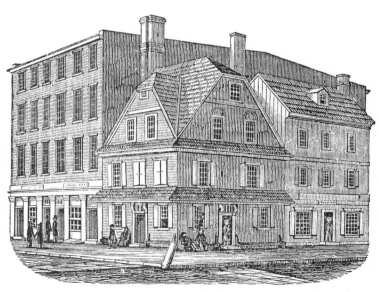

128. Old London Coffee House (built 1701), Front and Market Sts., Philadelphia, Penn., c. 1840. [12]

129. Slate-Roof House, residence of William Penn (built c. 1690: James Porteus, architect; demolished 1867), Third St., Philadelphia, Penn., c. 1853. [12]

130. Richard Townsend's House (built c. 1699), Chester, Penn. c. 1840. [12]

131. Isaac Potts' House, Revolutionary War headquarters of George Washington, Valley Forge, Penn., c. 1843. [12]

132. Letitia House (erected 1682), Letitia Court, Philadelphia, Penn., c. 1843. [12]

133. Betsey Williams House (erected 1770), Roger Williams Park, Providence, R.I., c. 1886. [16]

134. Old Indian House (built 1704; demolished 1848), Deerfield, Mass. [18]

135. Abbott House, near N. Main St., Providence, R.I., c. 1886.
[16]

136. Governor Arthur Fenner House (erected c. 1662), Cranston, R.I., c. 1886. [16]

137. *Rebecca Nourse House, Danvers, Mass., c. 1893. [9]*

138. *John Adams House, Quincy, Mass., c. 1893. [9]*

139. *Daniel Webster's birthplace, Salisbury, N.H., c. 1893. [9]*

140. *Minot House (built 1640; destroyed by fire 1874), Chicka-tawbut St., Neponset, Dorchester, Mass.* [41]

141. *Birthplace of Gilbert Stuart, North Kingstown, R.I., c. 1886.* [16]

Birth Place of
Benjamin West.

142. *Birthplace of Benjamin West, Springfield, Penn., c. 1853.* [15]

143. *General Huntington's House, Norwich, Conn., c. 1875.* [13]

144. *Birthplace of Israel Putnam (built 1744), Andover Rd. and Newburyport Tpk., Salem Village, Mass., c. 1875* [13]

145. Collins House, North Danvers, Mass., c. 1853. [15]

146. Governor Langdon's Mansion, Pleasant St., Portsmouth, N.H., c. 1875. [13]

147. Sir William Pepperell's House, Kittery Point, Maine, c. 1875. [13]

148. *General Anthony Wayne's House, Paoli, Penn., c. 1843.* [12]

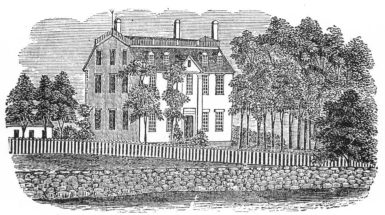

149. *Collins House, North Danvers, Mass., c. 1839.* [3]

150. *Captain Huddy's Mansion, Colt's Neck, N.J., c. 1840.* [2]

151. *Baker's Tavern, Hancock's Bridge, N.J., c. 1840.* [2]

152. *Garrison House, Pigeon Cove, Mass., c. 1849.* [35]

153. *Joseph Williams' House (erected c. 1680; demolished 1886), opposite Roger Williams Park, Providence, R.I.* [16]

154. Jones' School House (erected c. 1677; demolished 1879),
177 Main St., Pawtucket, R.I., c. 1875. [16]

155. First house built in Bethlehem, Penn., c. 1750. [12]

156. Birthplace of David Rittenhouse, Germantown, Penn., c.
1843. [12]

157. Elisha Brown House (built c. 1760), N. Main St., Providence, R.I., c. 1886. [16]

158. *John Hancock's House, Hull St., Boston, Mass., c. 1893.* [9]

159. *Washington's headquarters, Main St., Richmond, Va., c. 1893.* [9]

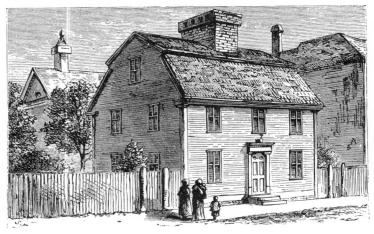

160. *Nathaniel Hawthorne's birthplace, Union St., Salem, Mass., c. 1875.* [13]

161. *Birthplace of Benjamin West, Springfield, Penn., c. 1843.* [12]

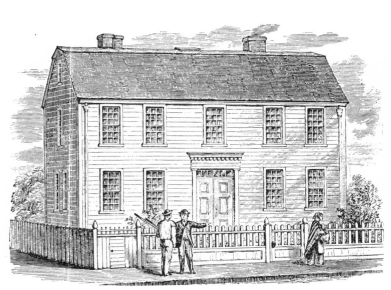

162. *Birthplace of General Knox (demolished 1881), Boston, Mass., c. 1756.* [41]

163. *Old house, Newcastle, Great Island, N.H., c. 1875.* [13]

52   HOUSES

164. Birthplace of President Monroe, Westmoreland County, Va., c. 1848. [38]

165. Andrew Jackson's birthplace, Mecklenburg County, N.C., c. 1893. [9]

166. A log cabin on the Auglaize River, Putnam County, Ohio, c. 1847. [22]

167. The Billop House (built c. 1680), Hylan Blvd., Staten Island, N.Y., c. 1848. [38]

168. Adams family residence, Quincy, Mass., c. 1848. [38]

169. *The Van Kleeck House (built 1702; demolished 1835), Poughkeepsie, N.Y., c. 1848. [38]*

170. *House in Scituate, Mass., c. 1874. [31]*

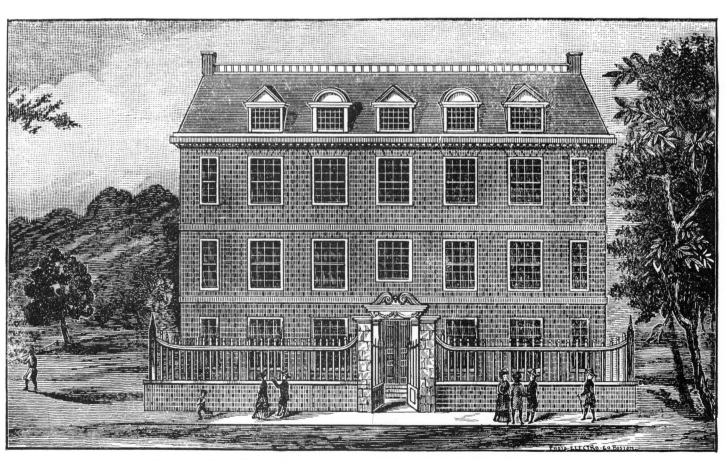

171. *Clark-Frankland House (built c. 1712: Robert Twelves, possible architect; demolished
c. 1832), Garden Ct. and Prince St., Boston, Mass. [41]*

172. *Hancock House (built 1740: Richard Munday, architect; demolished 1863; Beacon St., Boston, Mass. [25]*

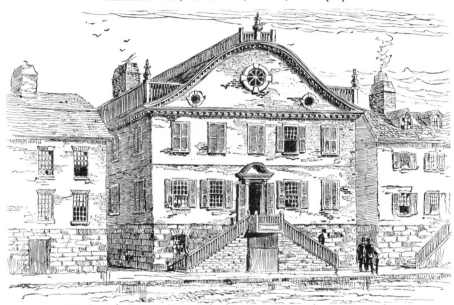

173. *Joseph Brown House (built c. 1774; Joseph Brown, architect), 50 S. Main St., Providence, R.I. c. 1886. [16]*

174. *The Chew House, Germantown, Penn., c. 1893. [9]*

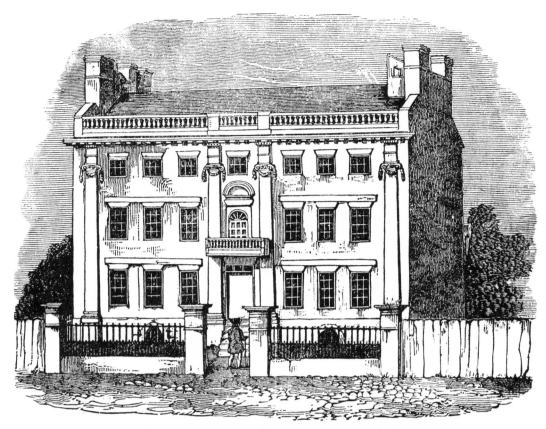

175. *The Hutchinson House (built c. 1686: Robert Twelves, possible architect; demolished c. 1832), North Sq., Boston, Mass. [41]*

176. *Hancock House (built 1740: Richard Munday, architect; demolished 1863; the headquarters of the New York State Historical Association in Ticonderoga, N.Y. is a reconstruction), Beacon St., Boston, Mass. [38]*

177. Vassall-Longfellow House (built 1760: Peter Harrison, architect), Cambridge, Mass., c. 1849. [35]

178. "Harris' Folly," High and Pearl Sts., Boston, Mass.

179. Residence of Rev. Jonathan Parsons, School St., Newburyport, Mass., c. 1839. [3]

180. Joanna Davis' House, Plymouth, Mass.. c. 1875. [13]

181. Chew House, Germantown, Penn., c. 1843, [12]

182. The oldest house in Bristol, R.I., c. 1886. [16]

183. Building in which the Declaration of Independence was
written, Philadelphia, Penn. [27]

184. Home of Francis Scott Key, Georgetown, Washington, D.C.,
c. 1893. [9]

185. Montpelier, home of President Madison, Orange County, Va., c. 1848. [38]

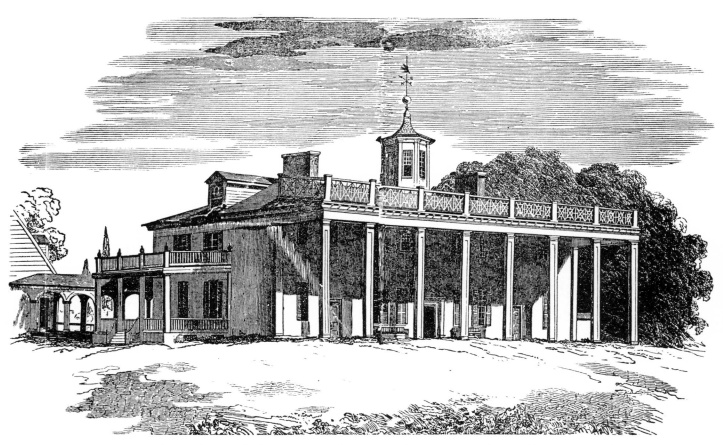

186. Mount Vernon (built 1774-1787: John Ariss, architect), Fairfax County, Va., c. 1848. [38]

187. Ford Mansion (built 1772: Thomas McBean, possible architect), Morristown, N. J., c. 1848. [38]

188. Governor Huntington's Mansion, Norwich, Conn., c. 1875. [13]

189. Duddington House (built c. 1795), N. Carolina Ave., Washington, D.C., c. 1886. [30]

190. *The White House (erected 1799: James Hoban, architect),*
1600 Pennsylvania Ave., Washington, D.C., c. 1886. [30]

191. *The White House, c. 1886.* [30]

192. *The White House, c. 1886.* [30]

*193. DeWolf-Colt House (built 1810: Russell Warren, architect),
Bristol, R.I., c. 1886. [16]*

194. Dorr Mansion (built 1809), Benefit St., Providence, R.I., c. 1886. [16]

195. Sears House (built 1816: Alexander Parris, architect), Boston Common, Boston, Mass., c. 1848. [38]

196. Leroy Pl., New York, N.Y.

197. *Federal town house, 23 Amity St., New York, N.Y. c. 1869.*
[39]

198. *[at right] House in which Lincoln died, Tenth St., Washington, D.C.,
c. 1893. [9]*

199. *Numbers 16-19 State St. (built 1815-1817: James O'Donnell, architect), New York, N.Y.,
c. 1864.*

200. *Residence of Joseph Bowers (Ithiel Town, architect), Northampton, Mass., c. 1830.*

201. *Residence of Col. Ralph Smith, Lodi, N.Y., c. 1876. [19]*

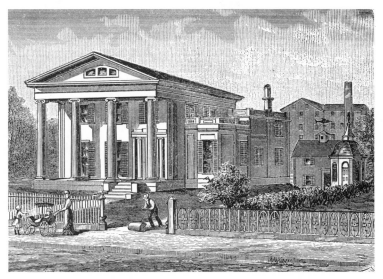

202. *Captain Collins' House, Bristol, R.I., c. 1886. [16]*

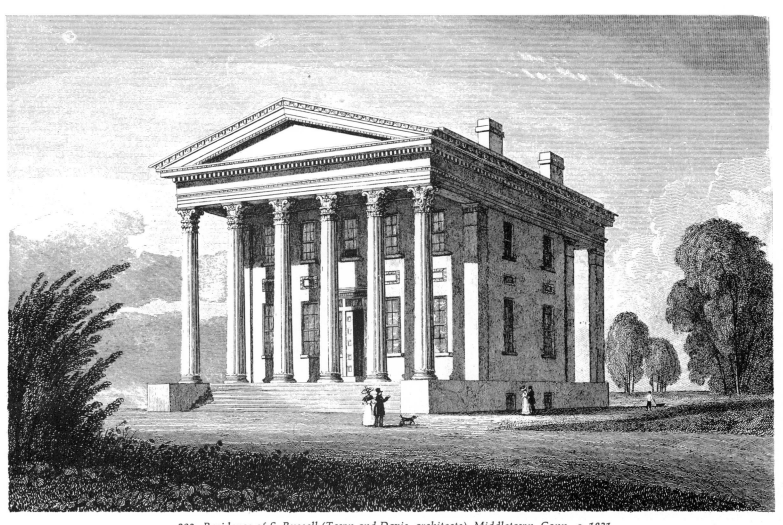

203. *Residence of S. Russell (Town and Davis, architects), Middletown, Conn., c. 1831.*

204. *Design for a rural Gothic farmhouse.*

205. *Gothic-revival cottage.*

206. Gothic-revival cottage.

207. Residence of Col. P. P. Lane, Norwood Heights, Ohio, c. 1876. [24]

208. Residence of S. C. Newhall, Highland Sq., Lynn, Mass., c. 1886. [21]

209. Residence of Ruggles S. Morse, Danforth and Park Sts., Portland, Maine, c. 1876. [14]

210. Large villa in Roman style (proposed design 1867: Gervase Wheeler, architect). [44]

211. *House on a farm (proposed design 1867: Gervase Wheeler, architect).* [44]

212. *Villa in English rustic style (proposed design 1867: Gervase Wheeler, architect).* [44]

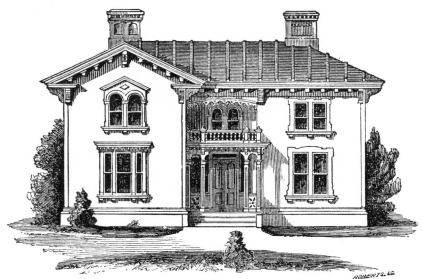

213. *Italian Cottage (proposed design 1867: Gervase Wheeler, architect).* [44]

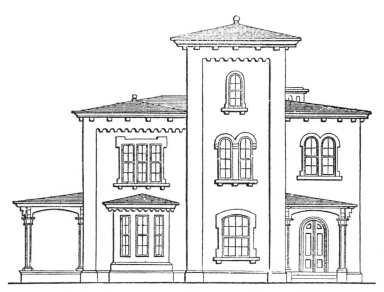

214. *Small symmetrical villa (proposed design 1867: Gervase Wheeler, architect).* [44]

215. *A villa (proposed design 1867: Gervase Wheeler, architect).* [44]

216. *Addition to an old house (proposed design 1867: Gervase Wheeler, architect).* [44]

217. *House in a row (proposed design 1867: Gervase Wheeler, architect).* [44]

218. *Gothic suburban villa (proposed design 1867: Gervase Wheeler, architect).* [44]

219. *Tenement house (proposed design 1867: Gervase Wheeler, architect).* [44]

220. *A residence to overlook the East River, N.Y., costing $4,000 complete (proposed design 1883: S. B. Reed, architect).* [36]

221. *Southern mansion (proposed design 1867: Gervase Wheeler, architect).* [44]

222. *Modern cottage costing $5,000 (proposed design 1883: S. B. Reed, architect), front elevation.* [36]

223. *Modern cottage costing $5,000 (proposed design 1883: S. B. Reed, architect), right elevation.* [36]

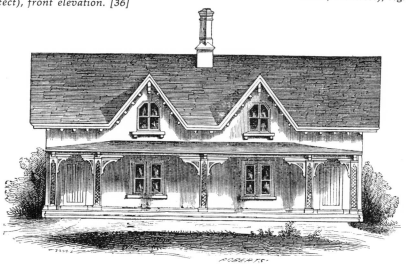

224. *Double cottage (proposed design 1867: Gervase Wheeler, architect).* [44]

225. *Cottage costing $750 (proposed design 1883: S. B. Reed, architect).* [36]

226. *Residence of Joshua S. Palmer, Portland, Maine, c. 1876.* [14]

227. Gatehouse and gates (proposed design 1867: Gervase Wheeler, architect). [44]

228. Suburban villa (proposed design 1867: Gervase Wheeler, architect). [44]

229. *William Wardwell residence, Bristol, R.I., c. 1886. [16]*

230. *Home of R. H. Goddard, Hope St., Providence, R.I., c. 1886.*
[16]

231. *Suburban cottage designed to cost $2,500.*

232. *Rural Gothic cottage design.*

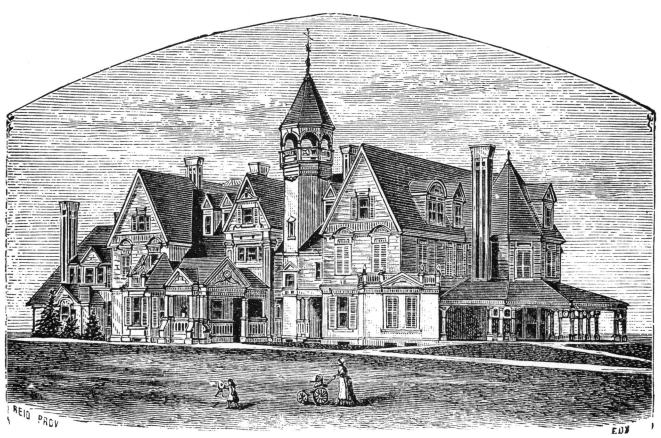

233. *Lorillard villa, Newport, R.I., c. 1886.* [16]

234. *Residence of John Anderton, Court St., Chicopee Falls, Mass., c. 1879.* [18]

235. *Residence of John Doty, Pavilion, N.Y., c. 1876.* [10]

236. *Villa mansion (proposed design 1867: Gervase Wheeler, architect).* [44]

237. *Residence of Enoch Heath, Pavilion, N. Y., c. 1876.* [10]

238. *Cottage, Newport, R.I., c. 1875.* [13]

239. *Charlotte Cushman's residence, Newport, R.I., c. 1875.* [13]

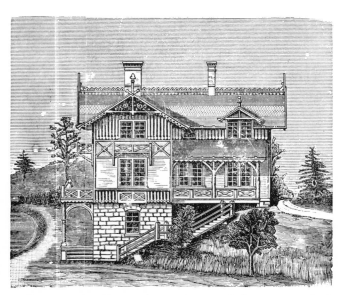

240. *Swiss cottage costing $1,600 (proposed design 1883: S. B. Reed, architect).* [36]

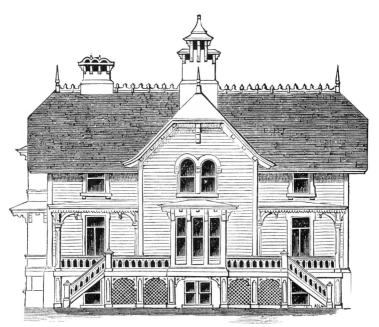

241. *Villa on the Hudson (proposed design 1867: Gervase Wheeler, architect), garden front.* [44]

242. *Villa on the Hudson (proposed design 1867: Gervase Wheeler, architect), entrance front.* [44]

243. *Country house in the North or South (proposed design 1867: Gervase Wheeler, architect).* [44]

244. *Cottage villa (proposed design 1867: Gervase Wheeler, architect).* [44]

245. Proposed design for a cottage to cost $1,800.

246. Proposed design for a small frame cottage to cost $2,000.

247. Residence of James Knapp, West Ave., South Norwalk, Conn.

248. Residence of James O. Inman, Burrillville, R.I., c. 1878. [20]

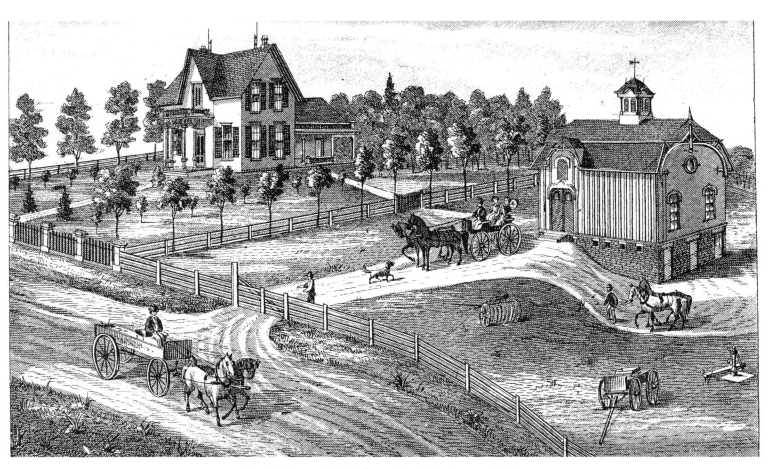

249. Residence of Oll Coomes, Franklin, Iowa, c. 1876.

250. Residence of R. P. Crafts, Holyoke, Mass., c. 1879. [18]

251. Residence of Charles H. Voorhis, Hackensack, N.J., c. 1876. [43]

252. Residence of A. B. Martin, High Rock Ave., Lynn, Mass., c. 1886. [21]

253. Residence of J. N. Smith, Ocean St., Lynn, Mass., c. 1886. [21]

254. Residence of State Senator William Johnson, Cayuga St., Seneca Falls, N.Y. c. 1876. [19]

255. Summer residence of John H. Keyser, Keyser's Island, near Norwalk, Conn.

256. The B. B. Knight mansion, Broad St., Providence, R.I., c. 1886. [16]

257. The English Legation Building, Connecticut Ave., Washington, D.C., c. 1886. [30]

258. Residence of James Sturdevant, Deer Hill Ave., Danbury, Conn.

259. Cottage orné (proposed design 1867: Gervase Wheeler, architect). [44]

260. *Lampson residence, Main St., Leroy, N.Y., c. 1876.* [10]

261. *Residence of Richard F. Hawkins, Franklin and Webster Sts., Springfield, Mass., c. 1879.* [18]

262. *Residence of J. F. Allyn, Holyoke, Mass., c. 1879.* [18]

263. *Residence of George H. Atwood, Anderson St., Hackensack, N.J., c. 1876.* [43]

264. *Residence of Benjamin Moses, Seneca Falls, N.Y., c. 1876.* [19]

265. *Residence of S. B. Allyn, Holyoke, Mass., c. 1879.* [18]

266. *House in Fairmount, N.J., c. 1876.* [43]

267. *Germantown villa, Phiiadelphia, Penn., c. 1876.* [26]

268. *Riverview, residence of O. H. Greenleaf (built 1873), Maple St., Springfield, Mass., c. 1879.* [18]

269. Residence of Emerson Gaylord, Chicopee, Mass., c. 1879. [18]

270. Residence of Henry Hoster, Fayette, N.Y., c. 1876. [19]

271. Residence of D. E. Partridge, Cayuga St., Seneca Falls, N.Y., c. 1876. [19]

272. *Country residence (proposed design 1867: Gervase Wheeler, architect).* [44]

273. *Cottage to cost $5,000 (proposed design 1883: S. B. Reed, architect), left elevation.* [36]

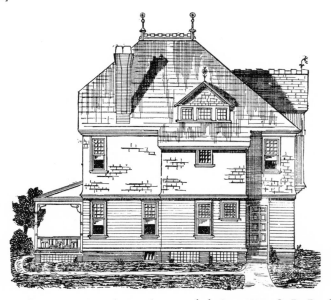

274. *Cottage to cost $5,000 (proposed design 1883: S. B. Reed, architect), rear elevation.* [36]

275. *Rustic parsonage (proposed design 1867: Gervase Wheeler, architect).* [44]

276. *Country cottage to cost $1,600 (proposed design 1883: S. B. Reed, architect).* [36]

277. *Suburban residence to cost $3,500 (proposed design 1883: S. B. Reed, architect).* [36]

278. *Suburban residence to cost $3,500 (proposed design 1883: S. B. Reed, architect).* [36]

279. *Little villa (proposed design 1867: Gervase Wheeler, architect).* [44]

280. *Farm house to cost $1,200 (proposed design 1883: S. B. Reed, architect).* [36]

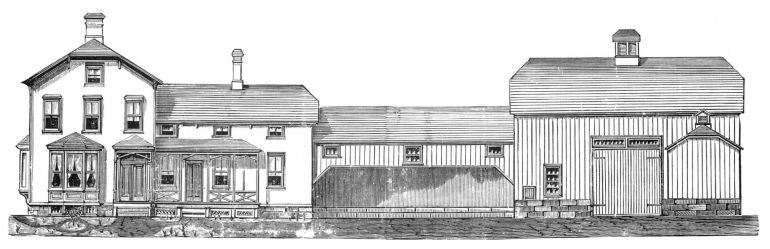

281. *Farm buildings costing $3,000 complete (modelled after the farm of Mr. George Thorpe in East Meriden, Conn.; proposed design 1883: S. B. Reed, architect).* [36]

282. *Residence of J. N. Buffum, Herbert St., Lynn, Mass., c. 1886.* [21]

283. *Residence of J. P. Woodbury, Nahant St., Lynn, Mass., c. 1886.* [21]

284. *Residence of Dr. James H. Holly, Warwick, N.Y., c. 1875.* [5]

285. Residence of John McAuslan, Elmwood, Providence, R.I., c. 1886. [16]

286. House in Fairmount, N.J., c. 1876. [43]

287. *Residence of James Barry, Ovid, N.Y., c. 1876.* [19]

288. *Abraham Batcheller House, Sutton, Mass., c. 1878.* [6]

289. *Residence of J. C. Newhall, Conway, Mass., c. 1879.* [18]

290. *Residence of David Odell, Tyre, N.Y., c. 1876.* [19]

291. *B. F. Peck farm, East Bethany, N.Y., c. 1876.* [10]

Worley & Bracher Lith Phila.

292. *Residences of Stephen Hoyt and Sons, nurserymen, New Canaan, Conn.*

293. *Major Caleb Stark farm, Dumbarton, N.H.*

294. *Residence of Aaron Wilson, Ovid, N.Y., c. 1876.* [19]

295. Residence of Nathaniel Seely, Waterloo, N.Y., c. 1876. [19]

296. Residence of R. M. Tucker, Conway, Mass., c. 1879 [18]

297. *Dodge homestead (erected c. 1750), Sutton, Mass., c. 1878.* [6]

298. *Dr. Artemis Bullard's place (built 1767), Sutton, Mass., c. 1878.* [6]

299. William King House (built 1722), Sutton, Mass., c. 1878. [6]

300. Residence of Oliver Chapin, Leyden, Mass., c. 1879. [18]

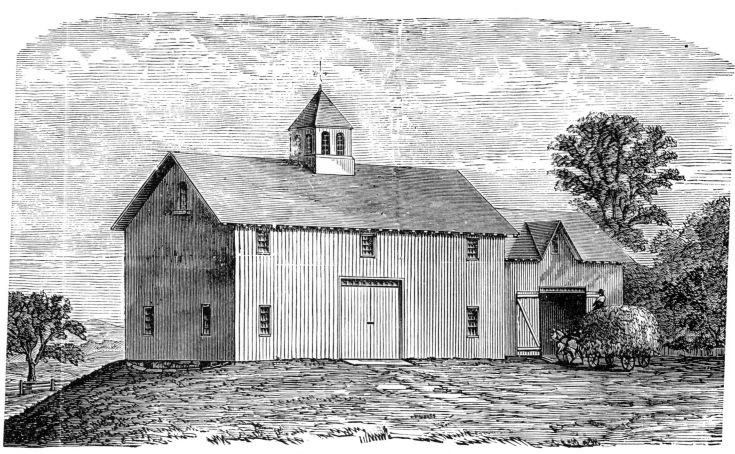

301. Design for a substantial farm barn.

302. Design for a grain and stock barn.

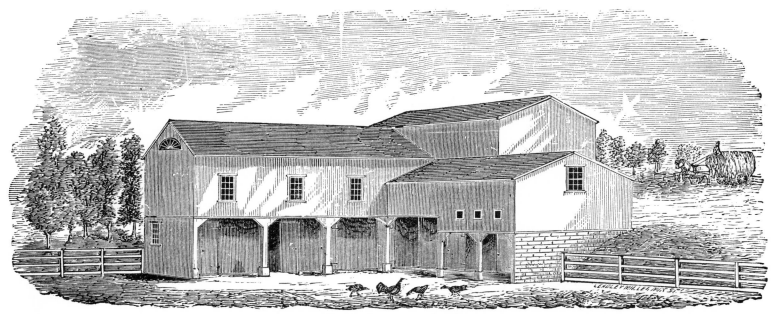

303. *Design for a convenient barn.*

304. *Carriage house and stable (proposed design 1858).* [23]

305. *Side-hill or cellar barn (proposed design 1858).* [23]

306. *Poultry house (proposed design 1858).* [23]

307. *Piggery (proposed design 1858).* [23]

308. First house in Greene County, Ohio (built 1798), c. 1847.
[22]

309. First hotel at Zanesville, Market and Second Sts., Zanesville,
Ohio. [22]

310. Williams' log cabin (built 1800), St. Clairsville, Ohio. [22]

311. Log cabin in Wisconsin, c. 1848. [38]

312. Thomas Lincoln's cabin, Farmington, Ill., c. 1886. [8]

313. Negro cabin in Virginia, c. 1848. [38]

314. *Harvard Hall (left center; built 1776: Governor Francis Bernard, architect), Harvard University, Cambridge, Mass., c. 1849.* [35]

315. *Wittenberg College, Springfield, Ohio, c. 1847.* [22]

316. *Ohio University, Athens, Ohio, c. 1847.* [22]

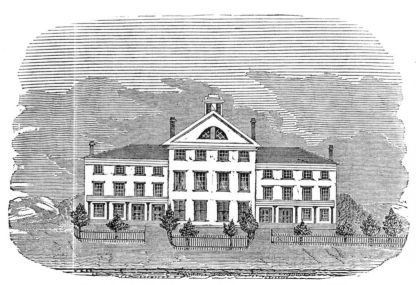

317. *Leicester Academy, Leicester, Mass., c. 1849.* [35]

318. *Old stone school house, Sutton, Mass., c. 1878.* [6]

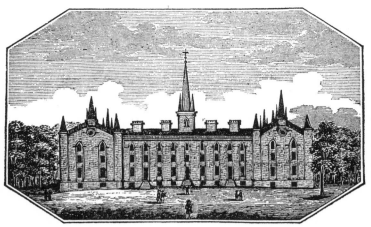

319. *Kenyon College, Gambier, Ohio, c. 1847.* [22]

320. *St. Xavier's College, Cincinnati, Ohio, c. 1847.* [22]

321. *Steubenville Female Seminary, Steubenville, Ohio, c. 1847.*
[22]

322. *Marietta College, Marietta, Ohio, c. 1847.* [22]

323. *Muskingum College, New Concord, Ohio, c. 1847.* [22]

324. *Whitworth Female College, Brookhaven, Miss., c. 1881.* [40]

325. *Weston Boarding School, a commercial and military institute for boys, Weston, Conn.*

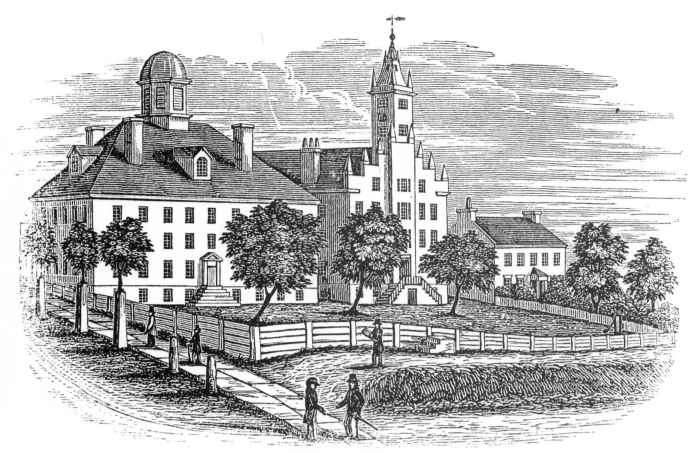

326. Jefferson College, Canonsburg, Penn., c. 1843. [12]

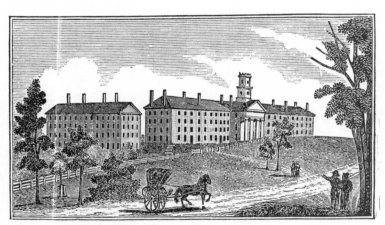

327. Amherst College, Amherst, Mass., c. 1839. [3]

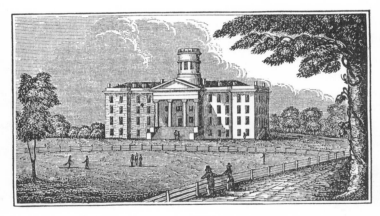

328. Pennsylvania College, Gettysburg, Penn., c. 1843. [12]

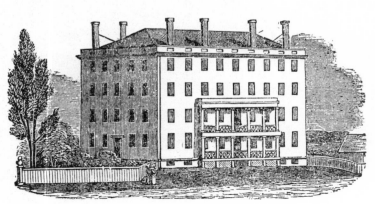

329. Mount Holyoke Female Seminary, South Hadley, Mass., c. 1839. [3]

330. Wesleyan Academy (established 1824), Wilbraham, Mass., c. 1839. [3]

331. *Presbyterian Theological Seminary, Princeton, N.J., c. 1848.* [38]

332. *Allegheny College, Meadville, Penn., c. 1843.* [12]

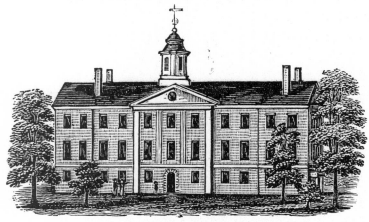

333. *Rutgers' College (constructed 1811), New Brunswick, N.J., c. 1840.* [2]

334. *Phillips Academy (built 1819), Andover, Mass., c. 1839.* [3]

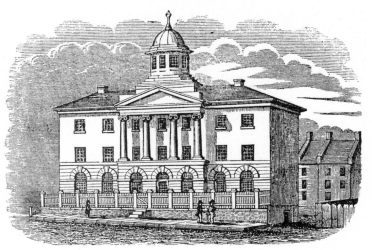

335. *Western University of Pennsylvania (erected 1830), Thirty-third St., Pittsburgh, Penn., c. 1843.* [12]

336. *Public School No. 17, Thirteenth St., New York, N.Y., c. 1848.* [4]

337. *Two-story school building (proposed design c. 1848: Town and Davis, architects).* [4]

338. *High school, President St., Providence, R.I., c. 1848.* [4]

339. *Westfield State Normal School, Westfield, Mass., c. 1848.* [4]

340. *Primary school (proposed design c. 1848: Public School Society of New York).* [4]

341. *High school, Hartford, Conn., c. 1848.* [4]

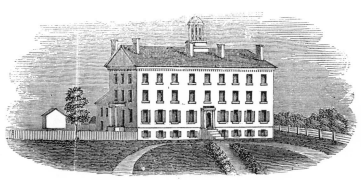

342. *Pennington Male Seminary (opened 1840), Pennington, N.J., c. 1842.* [2]

343. *Dickinson College, High St., Carlisle, Penn., c. 1843.* [12]

344. *Brown University, Providence, R.I., c. 1848.* [38]

345. *University Hall (center; built c. 1771: Robert Smith, architect), Brown University, Providence, R.I., c. 1886.* [16]

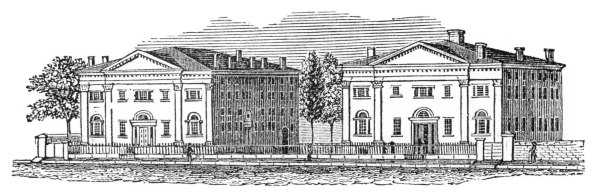

346. *University of Pennsylvania (built 1830), Ninth St., Philadelphia, Penn., c. 1843.* [12]

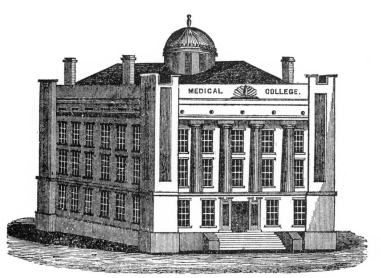

347. *Cleveland Medical College, Cleveland, Ohio, c. 1847.* [22]

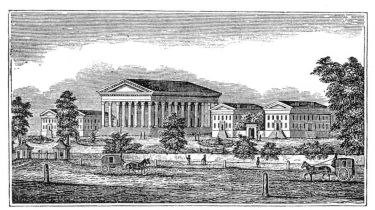

348. *Girard College (work in progress 1835: Thomas Walter, architect), Philadelphia, Penn.* [12]

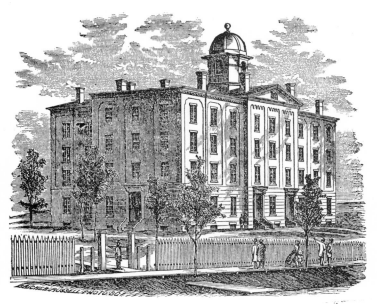

349. *Maine Wesleyan Seminary, Readfield, Maine, c. 1862.* [45]

350. *The old Boston Latin School, Bedford St., Boston, Mass., c. 1889.* [25]

351. *State Normal School, Westfield, Mass., c. 1879.* [18]

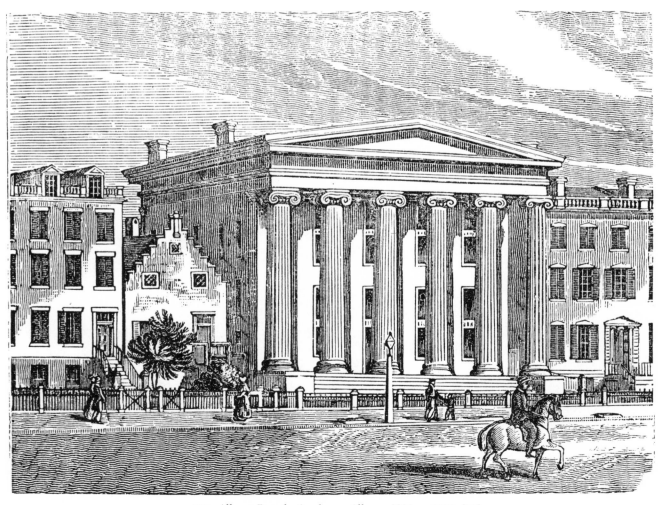

352. *Albany Female Academy, Albany, N.Y., c. 1848.* [38]

353. *Franklin College, Athens, Ga., c. 1854.* [15]

354. *The Collegiate School, Poughkeepsie, N.Y., c. 1848.* [38]

355. *District school, Hartford, Conn., c. 1848.* [4]

356. *District school, Windsor, Conn., c. 1848.* [4]

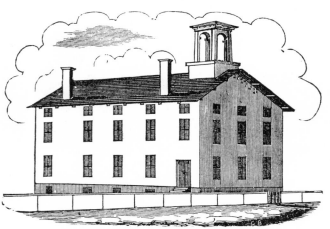

357. *High school, Parsonage St., Middletown, Conn., c. 1848.* [4]

358. *District school, Monroe, Mich., c. 1848.* [4]

359. *Grammar school, Providence, R.I., c. 1848.* [4]

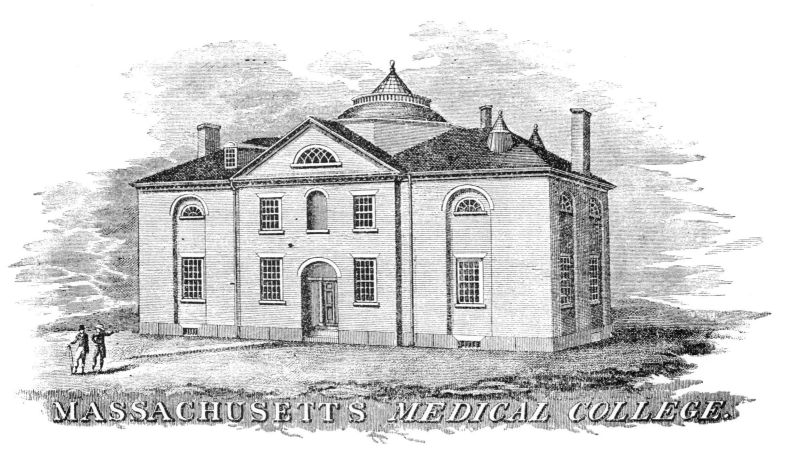

360. The Massachusetts Medical College, Mason St., Boston, Mass., c. 1816. [41]

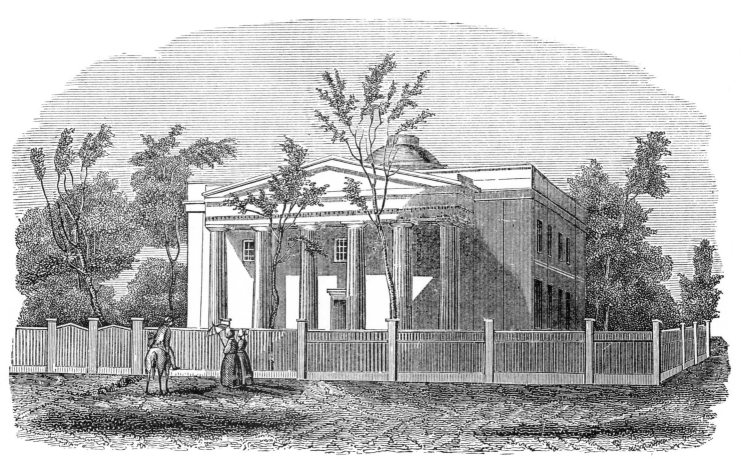

361. Medical College of Georgia (built 1834), Augusta, Ga., c. 1848. [38]

362. *Oglethorpe University (erected 1838), Medway, Ga., c. 1848.* [38]

363. *Ohio Wesleyan University, Delaware, Ohio, c. 1847.* [22]

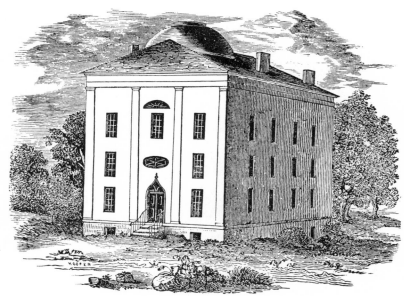

364. *Geneva Medical College, Geneva, N.Y., c. 1848.* [38]

365. *Washington County Seminary and Collegiate Institute, Fort Edward, N.Y., c. 1854.* [15]

366. *Starling Medical College and St. Francis Hospital (erected 1849: R. A. Sheldon, architect), State and Fifth Sts., Columbus, Ohio, c. 1873.* [42]

367. Yale College, New Haven, Conn., c. 1884. [1]

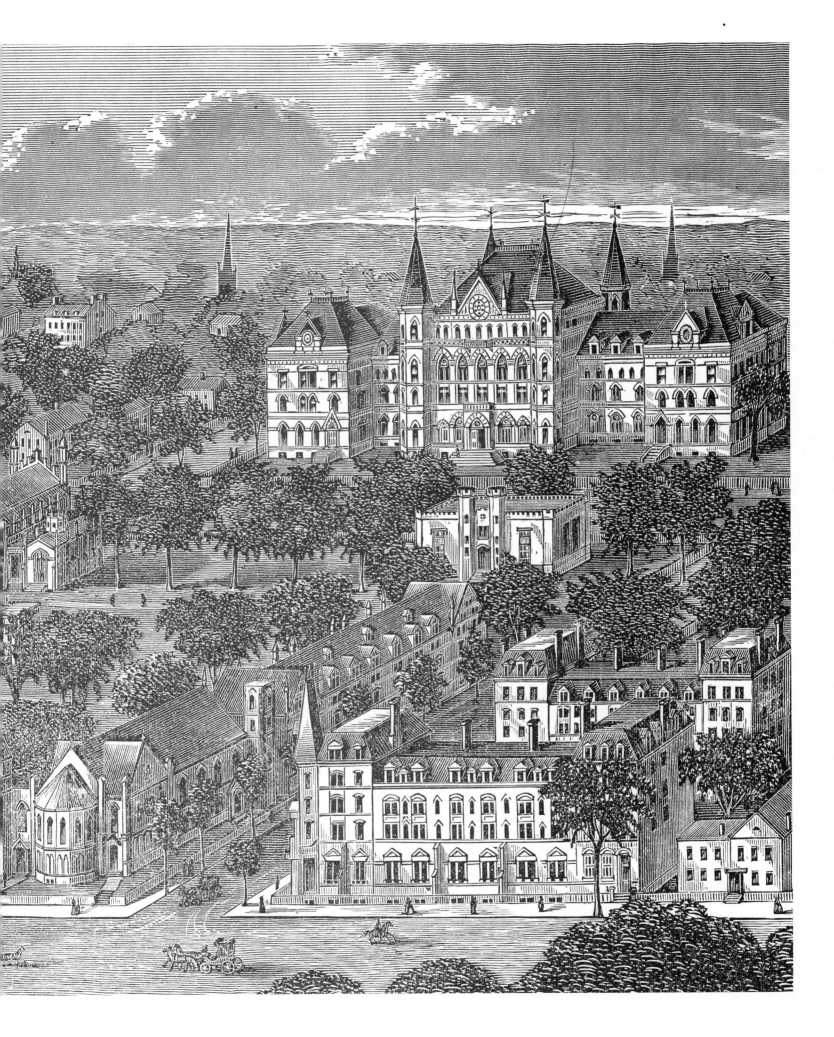

368. The Art Hall (erected 1868), Cincinnati Wesleyan College
for Young Women, Wesley Ave., Cincinnati, Ohio, c. 1876. [24]

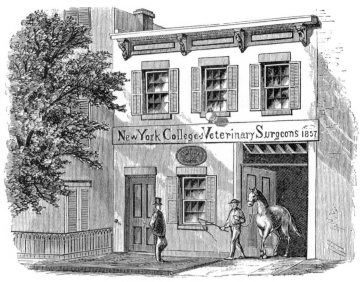

369. New York College of Veterinary Surgeons, 179 Lexington
Ave., New York, N.Y., c. 1869. [39]

370. The Harvard School of Veterinary Medicine (built c. 1885), Village and Lucas Sts.,
Boston, Mass., c. 1889. [25]

371. *Drew Seminary and Female College, Carmel, N.Y., c. 1881.* [40]

372. *Antioch College, Yellow Springs, Ohio, c. 1854.* [15]

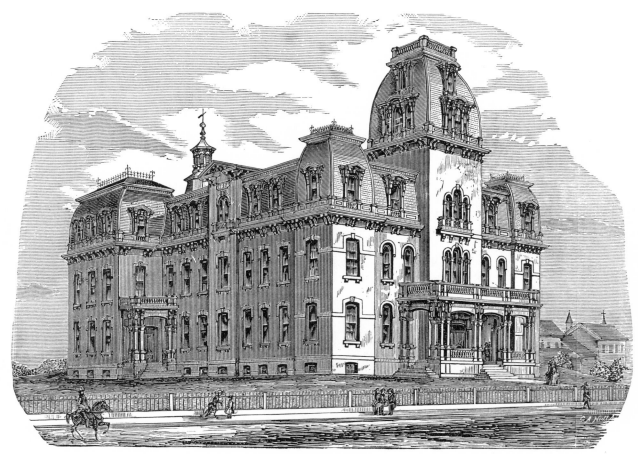

373. Point St. Grammar School, Providence, R.I., c. 1886. [16]

374. New York Free Academy (James Renwick, Jr., architect), Twenty-third St. and Lexington Ave., New York, N.Y., c. 1848. [4]

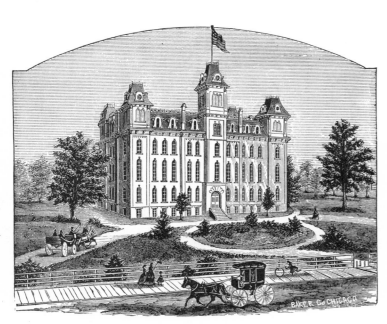

375. *Illinois Wesleyan University, Bloomington, Ill., c. 1881.* [40]

376. *Humboldt College, Humboldt, Iowa, c. 1876.*

377. *Academy of the Immaculate Conception, Davenport, Iowa, c. 1876.*

378. Amherst College, Amherst, Mass.

379. *School (proposed design c. 1848: Town and Davis, architects).* [4]

380. *District 6 school, Windsor, Conn., c. 1848.* [4]

381. *Cooper Union for the Advancement of Science and Art (built 1859: Frederick A. Peterson, architect), Astor Place, New York, N. Y., c. 1869.* [39]

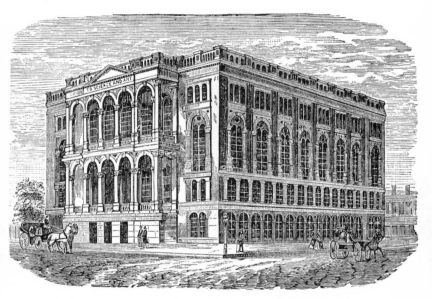

382. *Cooper Union for the Advancement of Science and Art (built 1859: Frederick A. Peterson, architect), Astor Place, New York, N.Y., c. 1884.* [1]

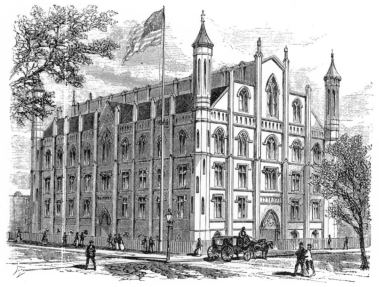

383. *New York Free Academy (James Renwick, Jr., architect), Twenty-third St. and Lexington Ave., New York, N.Y., c. 1869.* [39]

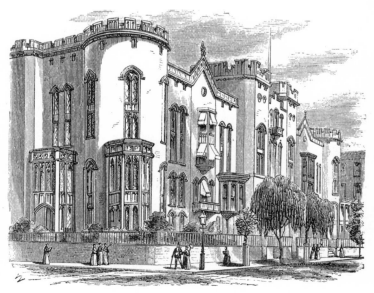

384. *Rutgers Female College, Fifth Ave. and Forty-second St., New York, N.Y., c. 1869.* [39]

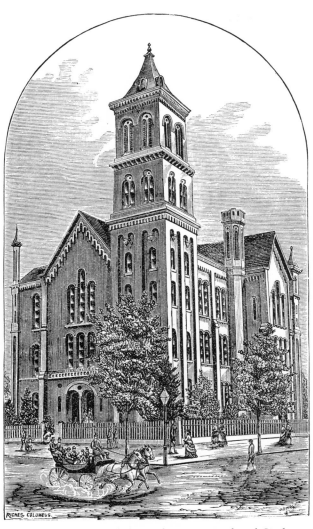

385. High school (opened 1862), Broad and Sixth Sts., Columbus, Ohio, c. 1873. [42]

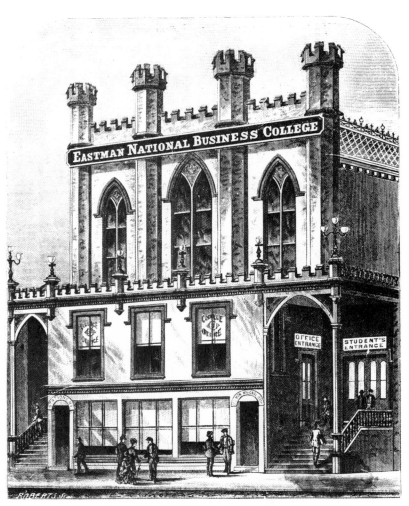

386. Eastman National Business College, Poughkeepsie, N.Y.

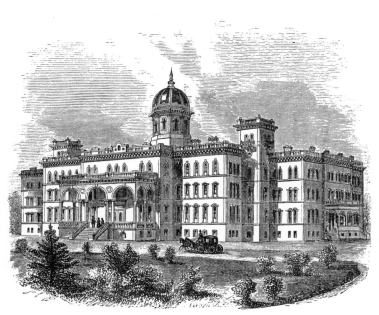

387. New York Institution for the Instruction of the Deaf and Dumb, One hundred sixty-second St., New York, N.Y., c. 1869. [39]

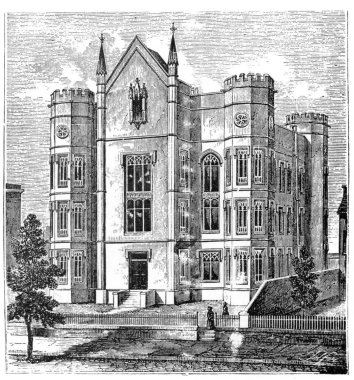

388. Hughes High School (built 1853), Fifth St., Cincinnati, Ohio, c. 1876. [24]

389. City Hall, Bangor, Maine, c. 1853. [15]

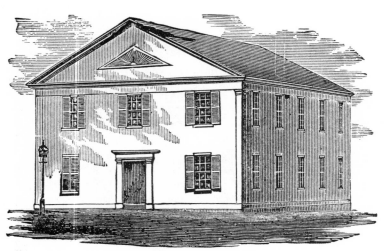

390. The old Town Hall (built 1714), Lynn, Mass. [21]

391. Marblehead Town Hall (erected 1727), Marblehead, Mass., c. 1893. [9]

392. *District Court House (erected 1820: George Hadfield, architect), Washington, D.C., c. 1886. [30]*

393. *Town Hall (erected 1851: William F. Pratt, architect), Northampton, Mass., c. 1854. [15]*

394. Boston City Hall (dedicated 1865: Bryant and Gilman, architects), School St., Boston, Mass., c. 1889. [25]

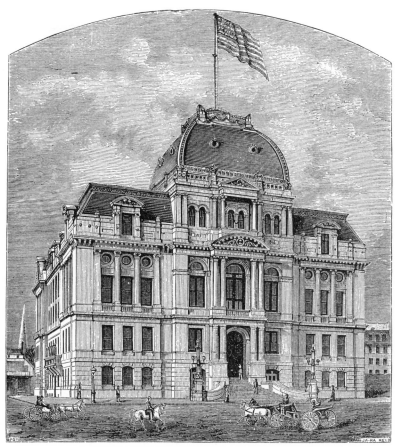

395. City Hall (built 1875), Exchange Pl., Providence, R.I., c. 1886. [16]

396. Portland City Hall, Congress St., Portland, Maine, c. 1876. [14]

397. City Hall (built 1845-46; re-modeled 1872-73), Fall River, Mass., c. 1877. [33]

398. City Hall, Dwight and High Sts., Holyoke, Mass., c. 1879. [18]

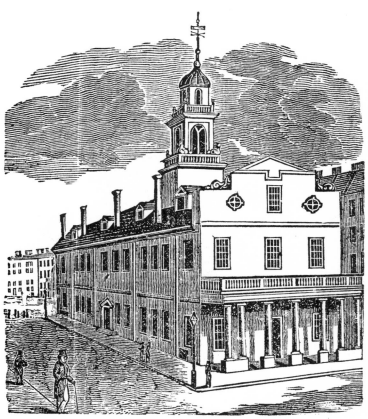

399. *Old State House (built 1711: Robert Twelves, possible architect), State St., Boston, Mass., c. 1839.* [29]

400. *State House, N. Main St., Providence, R.I., c. 1886.* [16]

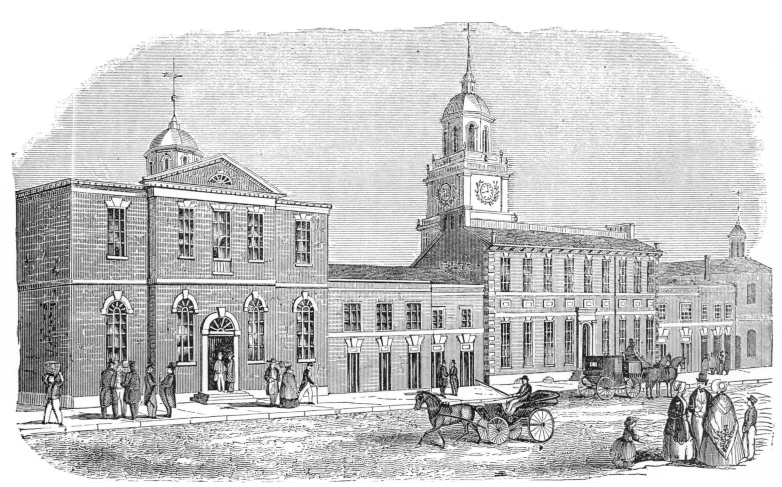

401. *Independence Hall (built 1732-1755: Edmund Woolley, architect), Philadelphia, Penn., c. 1848.* [38]

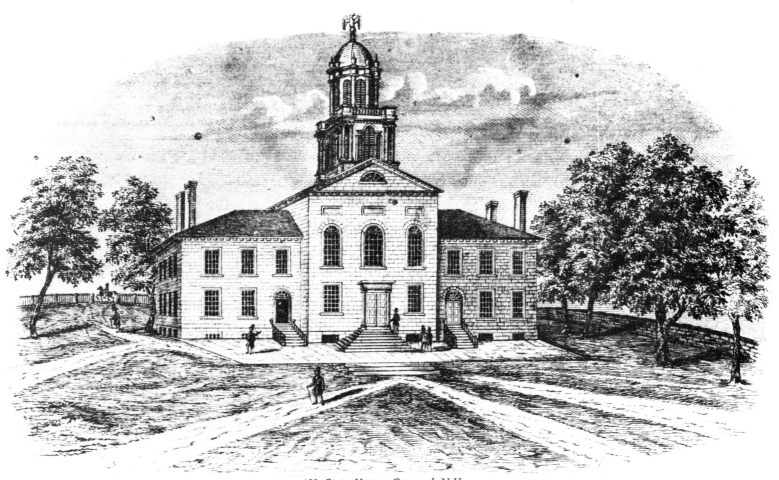

402. *State House, Concord, N.H.,*

403. *The first state buildings at Columbus,* LEFT: *the Old State Offices (erected 1815; demolished 1857);* RIGHT: *the Old State House (erected 1814; destroyed by fire 1852), High and State Sts., Columbus, Ohio.* [42]

404. *State House, Concord, N.H., c. 1876.* [27]

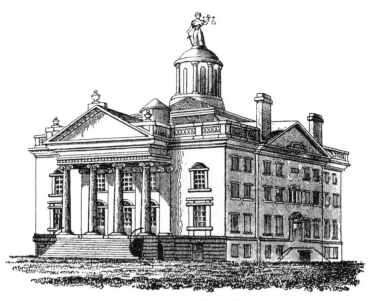

405. *State Capitol (erected 1805: Philip Hooker, architect), Albany, N.Y.*

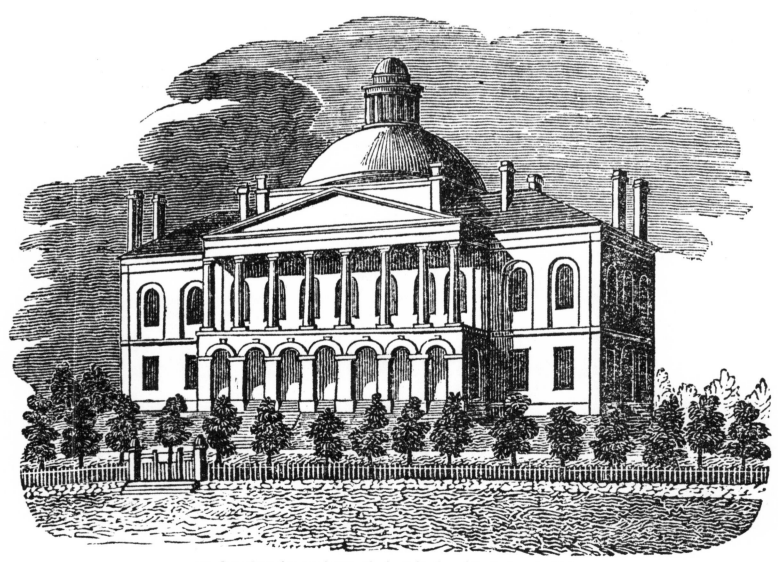

406. *State Capitol (erected 1829: Charles Bulfinch, architect), Augusta, Maine.*

407. *State Capitol (built 1833-1840: Town and Davis and David Paton, architects), Raleigh, N.C., c. 1848. [38]*

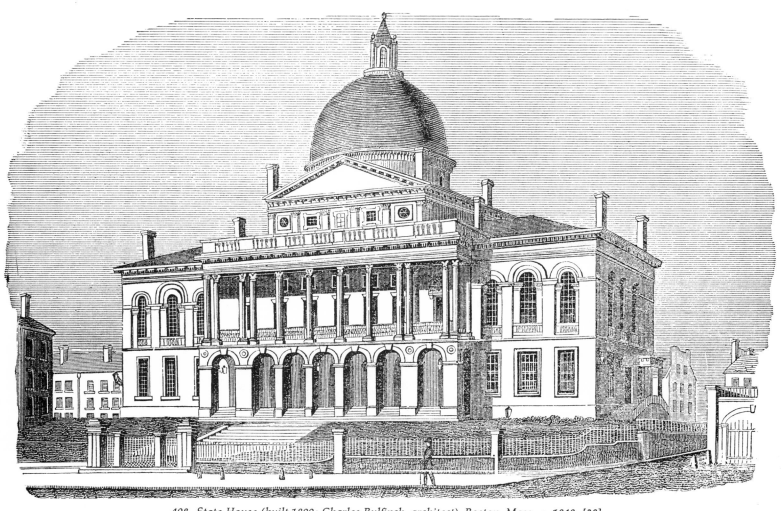

408. *State House (built 1800: Charles Bulfinch, architect), Boston, Mass., c. 1848. [38]*

409. County buildings, Mount Holly, N.J., c. 1868. [2]

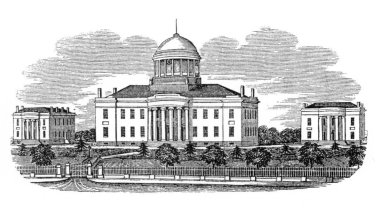

410. State Capitol (erected 1820: Stephen Hills, architect), Harrisburg, Penn., c. 1843. [12]

411. Old State House (built 1801), Chillicothe, Ohio, c. 1847. [22]

412. State House, Trenton, N.J., c. 1868. [2]

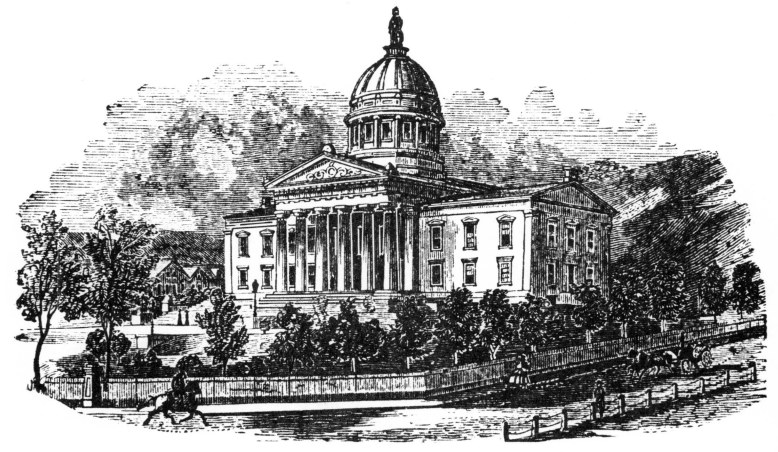

413. State Capitol (erected 1837: Ammi B. Young, architect), Montpelier, Vt.

414. *Old State Capitol (erected 1827-1831: Ithiel Town, architect), New Haven, Conn.*

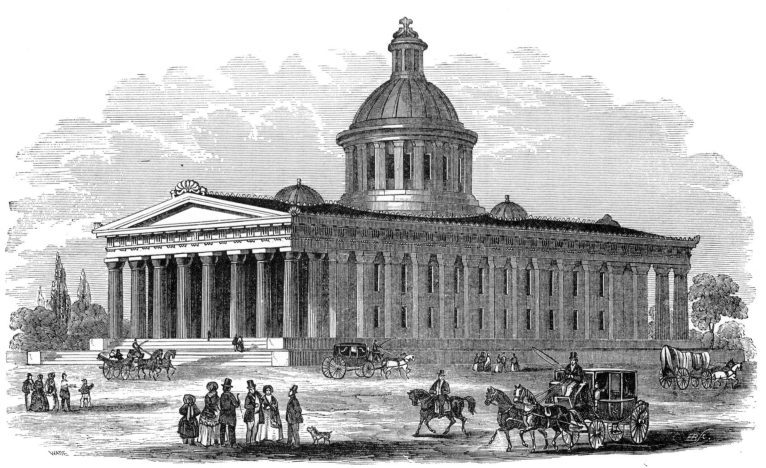

415. *State Capitol (erected 1834: Town and Davis, architects; modelled after the Parthenon),*
Indianapolis, Ind., c. 1854. [15]

416. *State Capitol (built 1789: Thomas Jefferson, architect), Richmond, Va., c. 1848. [38]*

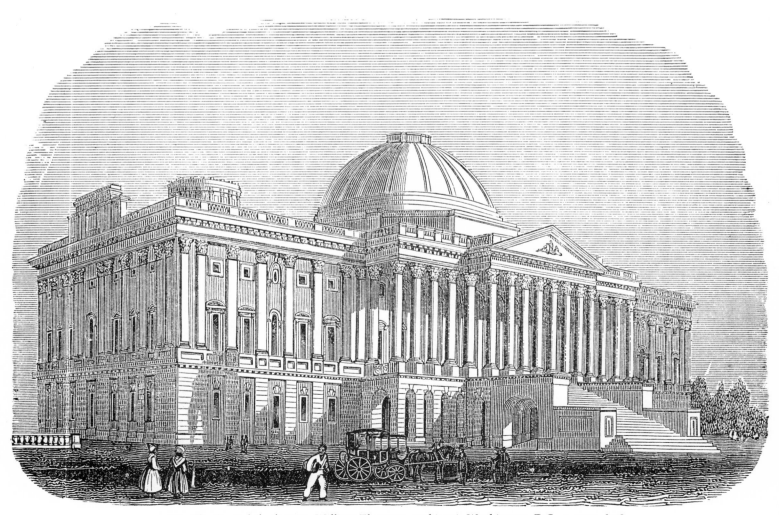

417. *The Capitol (built 1793: William Thornton, architect), Washington, D.C., c. 1848. [38]*

418. Statehouse, Milledgeville, Ga., c. 1848. [38]

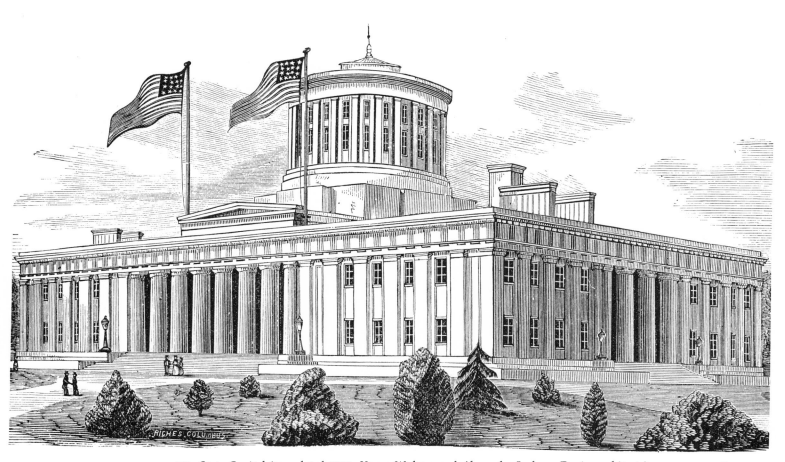

*419. State Capitol (completed 1861: Henry Walters and Alexander Jackson Davis, architects),
Columbus, Ohio, c. 1873. [42]*

420. *State Capitol, Des Moines, Iowa, c. 1893.* [46]

421. *State Capitol, Salem, Ore., c. 1893.* [46]

422. *State Capitol, Lansing, Mich., c. 1876.* [27]

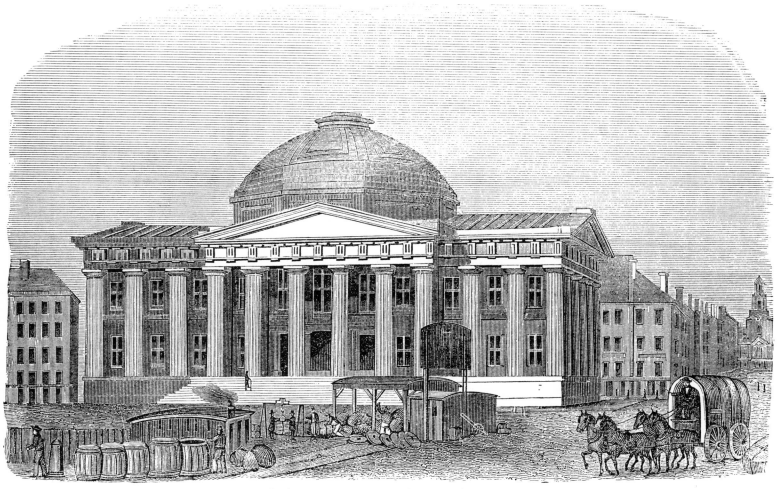

423. *Custom House (built 1837-1847: Ammi B. Young, architect), Boston, Mass., c. 1848.* [38]

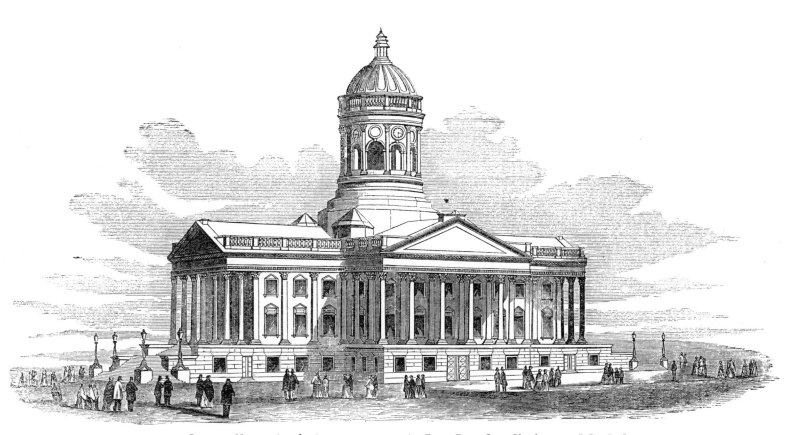

424. *Custom House (work in progress 1854), East Bay St., Charleston, S.C.* [15]

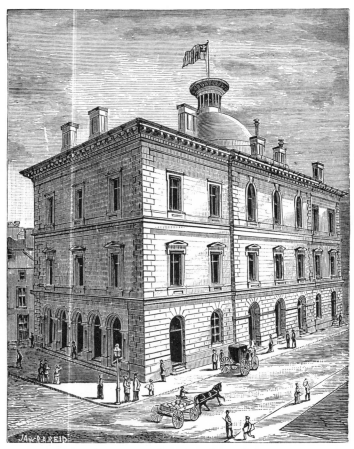

425. *Providence post office, Providence, R.I., c. 1886.* [16]

426. *Post office, Middle and Exchange Sts., Portland, Maine, c. 1876.* [14]

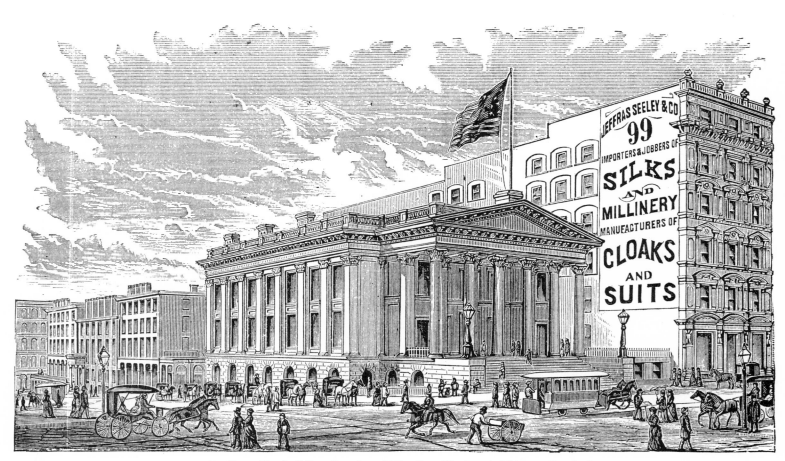

427. *Post office building, Fourth and Vine Sts., Cincinnati, Ohio, c. 1876.* [24]

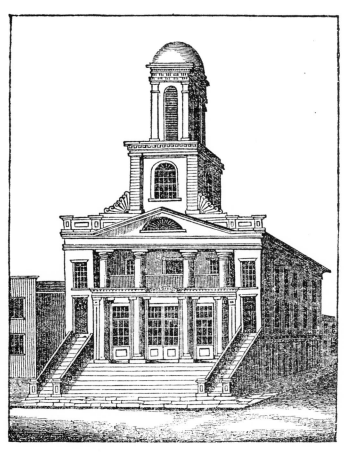

428. *Buffalo post office, Washington and Seneca Sts., Buffalo, N.Y.*

429. *Post office, Chestnut St., Philadelphia, Penn., c. 1876. [26]*

430. *United States Post Office and Sub-Treasury Building (opened c. 1872), Post Office Sq.,*
Boston, Mass., c. 1889. [25]

431. *Jail, Old York, Maine, c. 1875.* [13]

432. *Ohio Penitentiary, Columbus, Ohio, c. 1847.* [22]

433. *Old Jail, Park Row, New York, N.Y.*

434. *Eastern State Penitentiary (built 1829: John Haviland, architect), near Fairmount, Penn., c. 1848.* [38]

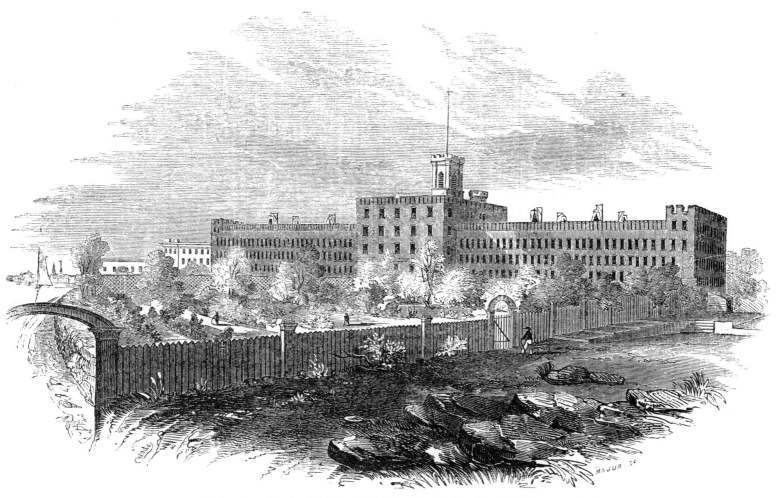

435. *Penitentiary, Blackwell's Island (Welfare Island), New York, N.Y., c. 1853. [15]*

436. *Ohio Penitentiary, Columbus, Ohio, c. 1847. [22]*

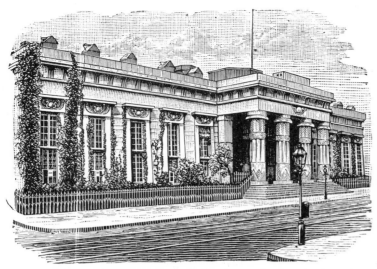

437. *The Tombs (City Prison; built 1838: John Haviland, architect; dismantled 1938), Centre and Leonard Sts., New York, N.Y., c. 1885.* [11]

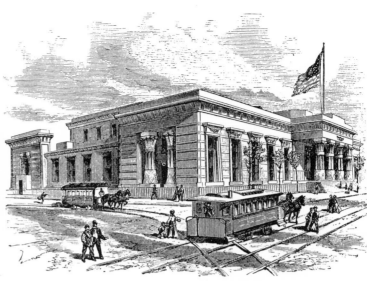

438. *The Tombs, c. 1869.* [39]

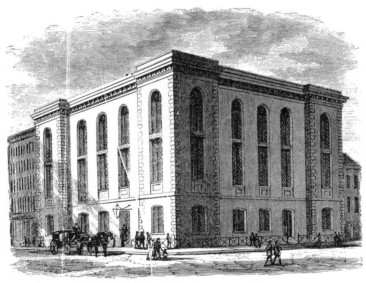

439. *New York County Jail (built 1862), Ludlow St. and Essex Market Pl., New York, N.Y., c. 1869.* [39]

440. *Moyamensing Prison (built 1835: Thomas U. Walter, architect), Tenth and Eleventh Sts., Philadelphia, Penn., c. 1843.* [12]

441. *Moyamensing Prison, c. 1876.* [26]

442. *Prisoners' cells in the penitentiary on Blackwell's (now Welfare) Island, New York, N.Y., c. 1891.* [7]

443. *The County Jail, Lowell, Mass., c. 1874.* [31]

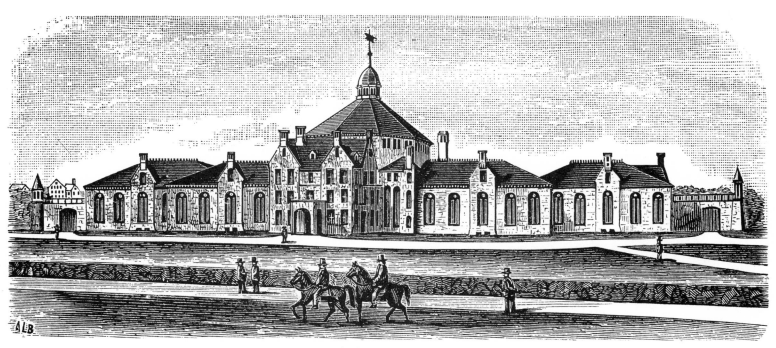

444. *State Prison (built 1878), Cranston, R.I., c. 1886.* [16]

445. *Thirty-third precinct police station, Town Hall, Third and Washington Aves., Morrisania, Bronx, N.Y. c. 1885. [11]*

446. *Thirty-second precinct police station (built 1874), Tenth Ave. and 152 St., New York, N. Y., c. 1885. [11]*

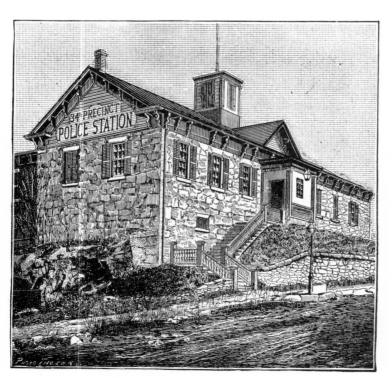

447. *Thirty-fourth precinct police station, 1925 Bathgate Ave., Bronx, N.Y., c. 1885. [11]*

448. *Eleventh precinct police station, Sheriff and Houston Sts., New York, N.Y., c. 1885. [11]*

449. *Fourteenth precinct police station and House of Detention, 205 Mulberry St., New York, N.Y., c. 1885.* [11]

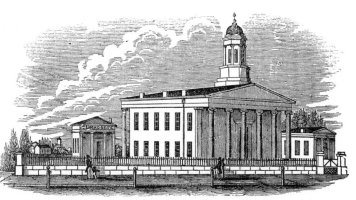

450. *County buildings (built 1839), South Trenton, N.J., c. 1868.* [2]

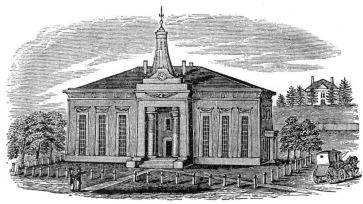

451. *Courthouse (built 1837: John Haviland, architect), Newark, N.J., c. 1868* [2]

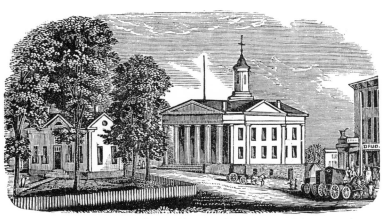

452. *Courthouse, Newton, N.J., c. 1868.* [2]

453. *Courthouse, Flemington, N.J., c. 1868.* [2]

454. *Courthouse, Woodbury, N.J.* [2]

455. *Courthouse (built c. 1800), Freehold, N.J., c. 1868.* [2]

456. *Old Courthouse (erected 1707; demolished c. 1830), Market and Second Sts., Philadelphia, Penn. [12]*

457. *Courthouse, Newton, N.J., c. 1842. [2]*

458. *Williamsburg Courthouse (built 1770: Robert Smith, architect), Williamsburg, Va., c. 1893. [9]*

459. *Courthouse (John Chislett, architect; burned 1882), Pittsburgh, Penn., c. 1843. [12]*

460. *Courthouse (erected 1798), Somerville, N.J., c. 1868. [2]*

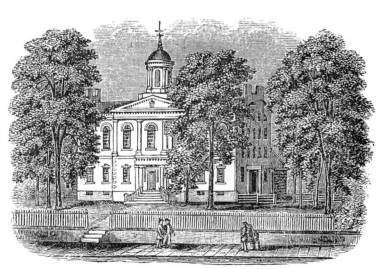

461. *Courthouse, Morristown, N.J., c. 1868. [2]*

462. Courthouse and jail, Waterloo, N.Y., c. 1876. [19]

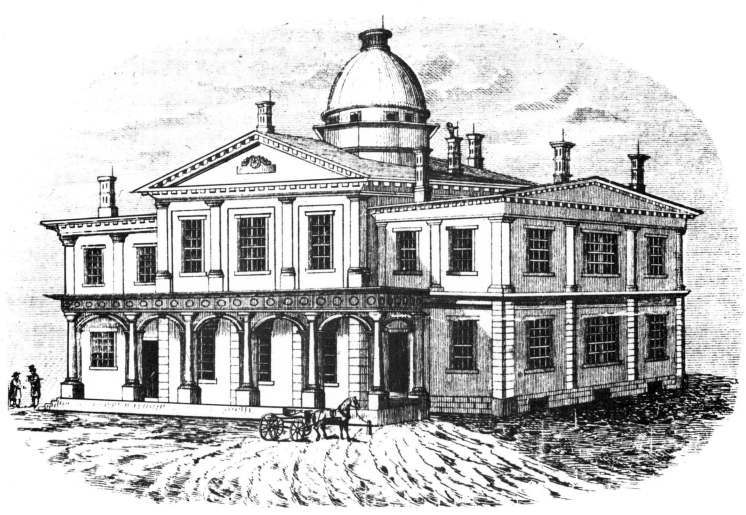

463. Courthouse, Concord, N.H.

464. Courthouse (built 1784), State St., New London, Conn., c. 1875. [13]

465. Courthouse (built 1821), Springfield, Mass., c. 1879. [18]

466. County Courthouse, Hackensack, N.J., c. 1876. [43]

467. Courthouse, High and Mound Sts., Columbus, Ohio, c. 1873. [42]

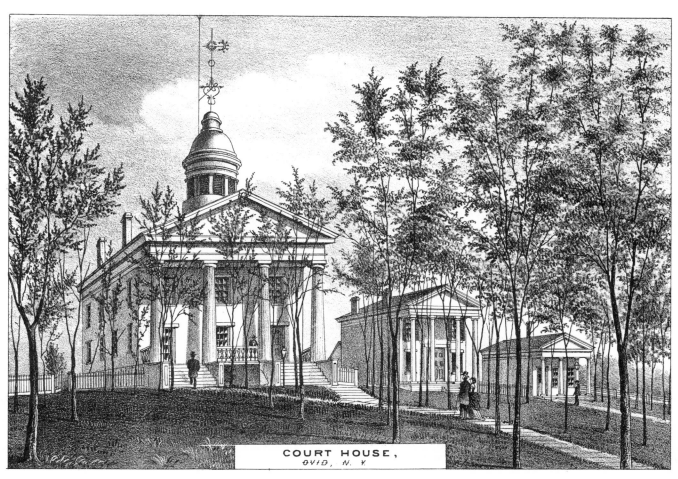

COURT HOUSE,
OVID, N. Y.

468. Courthouse, Ovid, N.Y., c. 1876. [19]

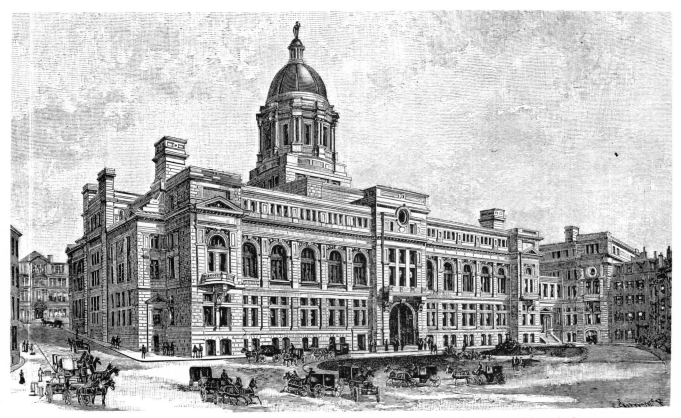

469. *Suffolk County Courthouse (work in progress 1889), Pemberton Sq., Boston, Mass.* [25]

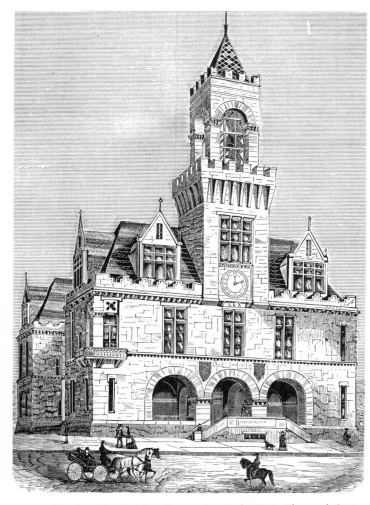

470. *Hamden County Courthouse (erected 1874), Elm and State Sts., Springfield, Mass., c. 1879.* [18]

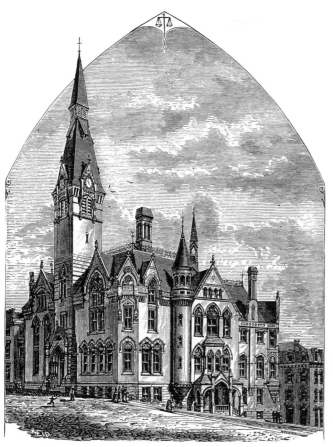

471. *County Courthouse (built 1877), Benefit and College Sts., Providence, R.I., c. 1886. [16]*

472. *Courthouse, Algona, Iowa, c. 1876.*

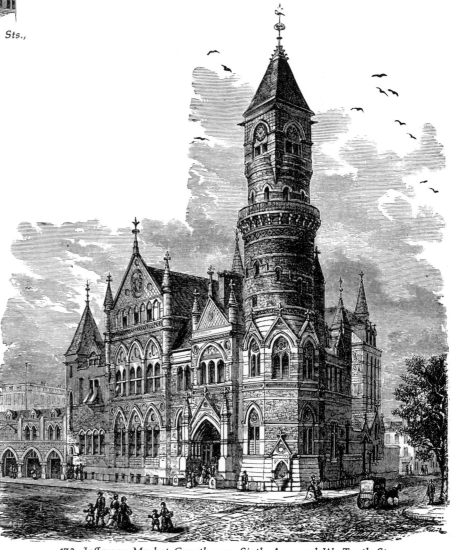

473. *Jefferson Market Courthouse, Sixth Ave. and W. Tenth St., New York, N.Y., c. 1885. [11]*

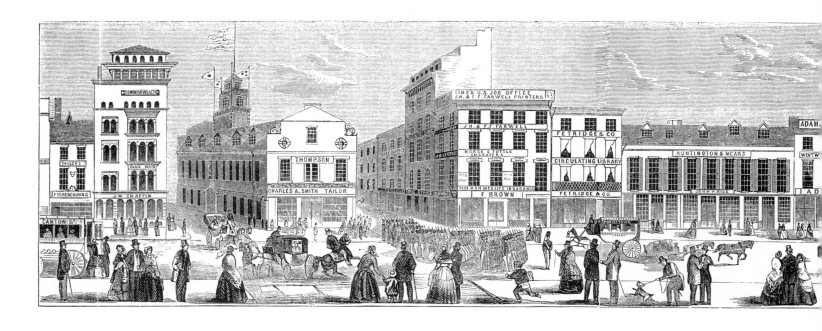

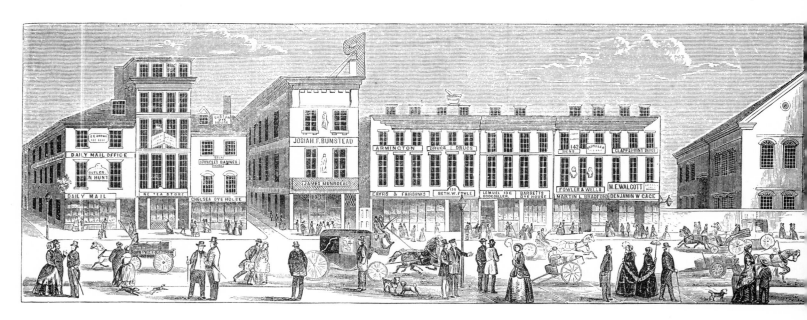

474, 475, 476. *Grand Panoramic View of the East Side of Washington St., Boston, Mass.,
Commencing at the corner of State St. and extending to No. 206, c. 1855.* [15]

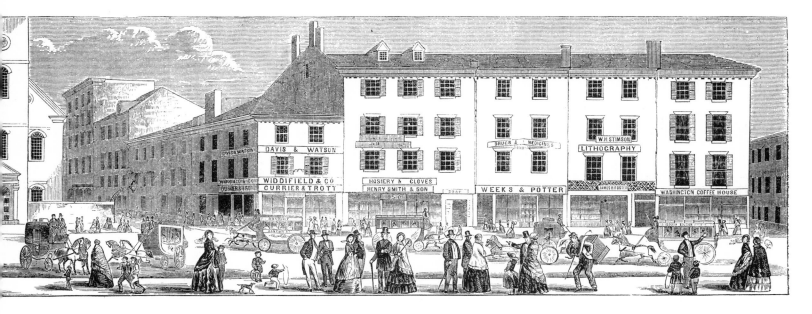

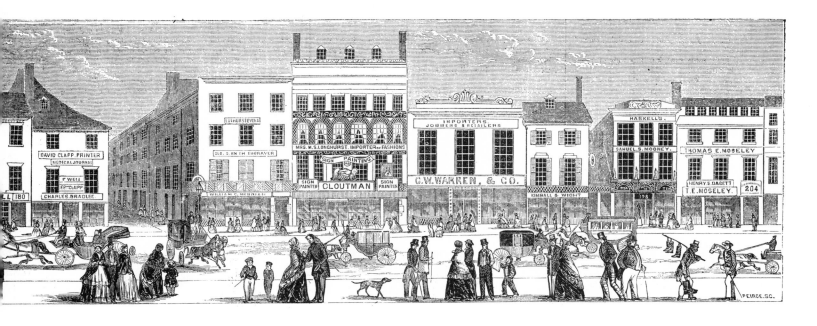

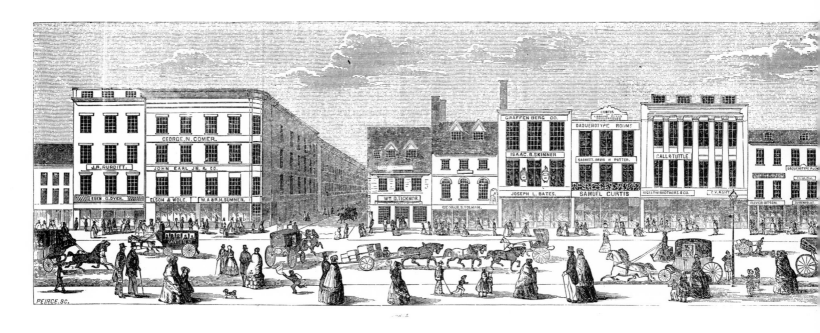

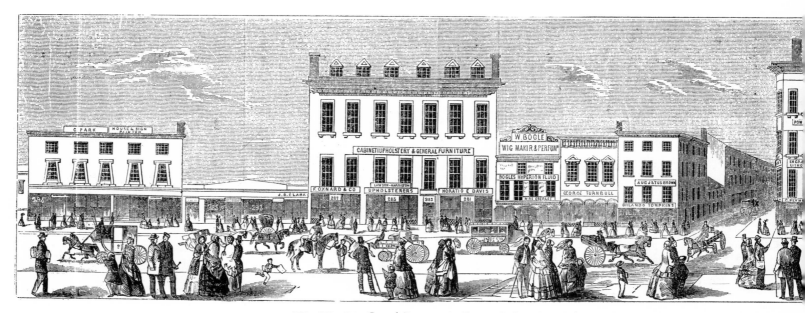

477, 478, 479. *Grand Panoramic View of the West Side of Washington St., Boston, Mass.,
Commencing at the corner of Court St., and extending to No. 295 above Winter St., c. 1855.*

[15]

480. Bridgeport Wood Finishing Co., 40 Bleecker St., New York, N.Y., c. 1884. [1]

481. *De Young's Fancy Store, Philadelphia, Penn.*

482. *H. and E. M. McCormick Hat, Cap and Fur Store, Batavia, N.Y., c. 1876.* [10]

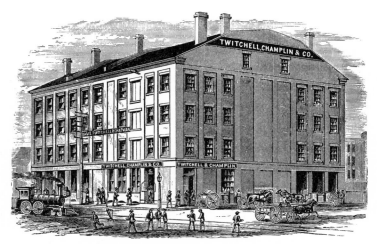

483. *Warehouses, Commercial St., Portland, Maine, c. 1876.* [14]

484. *Joy Building (built 1808), Washington St., Boston, Mass., c. 1830.* [41]

485. J. and J. Harper, Printers, 82 Cliff St., N.Y., c. 1825.

486. Shops, Boston, Mass.

487. J. A. Clark's Jewelry Store, 90 Main St., Batavia, N.Y., c. 1876. [10]

488. *Towsley House Hotel, Waterloo, N.Y., c. 1876.* [19]

489. *Presbyterian Board of Publication, Chestnut St., Philadel-*
phia, Penn., c. 1876. [26]

490. *New York Stock Exchange, 10 Broad St., New York, N.Y.,*
c. 1869. [39]

491. *Lampson House Hotel, Main St., Leroy, N.Y., c. 1876.* [10]

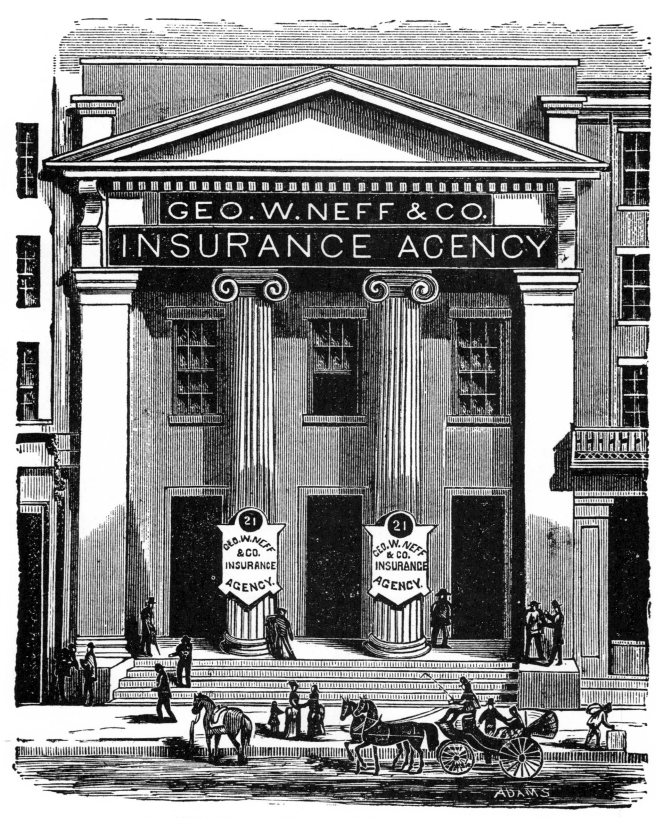

492. *George W. Neff Insurance Office, 21 W. Third St., Cincinnati, Ohio, c. 1876.* [24]

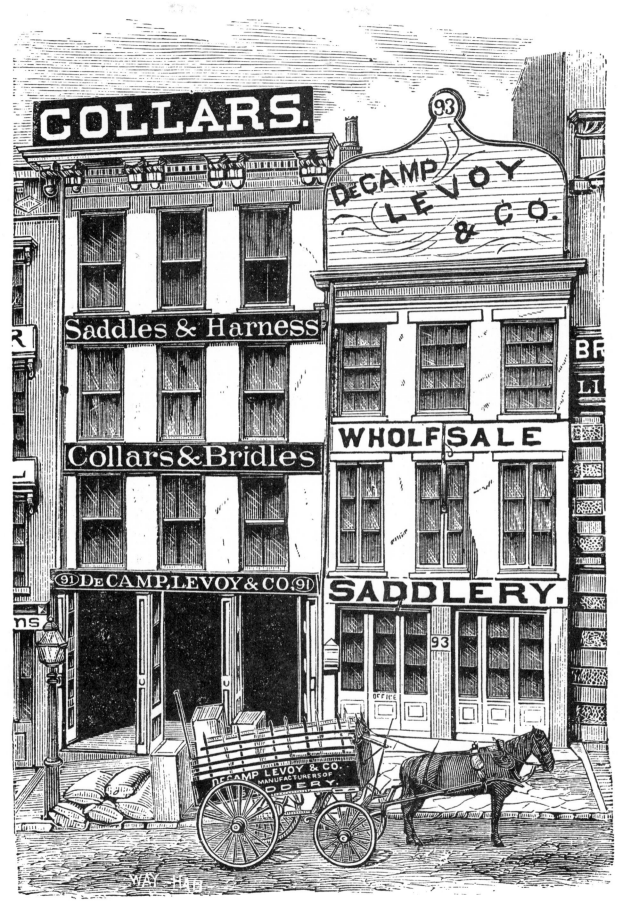

493. *DeCamp, Levoy and Co., 91–93 Main St., Cincinnati, Ohio, c. 1876.* [24]

494. *Chestnut St., Philadelphia, Penn., south side from Seventh to Eighth Sts., c. 1879.*

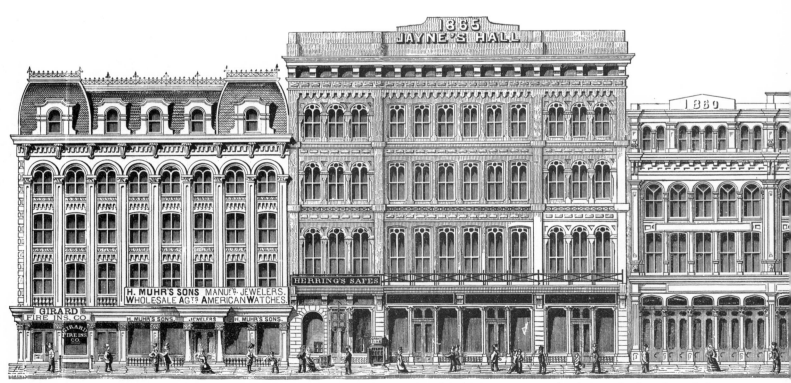

495. *Chestnut St., Philadelphia, Penn., north side from Sixth to Seventh Sts., c. 1879.*

*496. John Wanamaker's Clothing House, Market St., Philadel-
phia, Penn., c. 1876. [26]*

*497. Typical pawnshop, New York, N.Y., c. 1891.
[7]*

498. Business block, Warwick, N.Y., c. 1875. [5]

499. *T. F. Woodward's Boot and Shoe Store, 74 Main St., Batavia, N.Y., c. 1876.* [10]

500. *G. G. Elmore, Wholesale and Retail Druggist, 92 Main St., Batavia, N.Y., c. 1876.* [10]

501. *Turner and Jones meat market, 51 and 53 Main St., Batavia, N.Y., c. 1876.* [10]

502. *Orange County Press, 50 North St., Middletown, N.Y., c. 1875.* [5]

503. Broadway and Thirty-first St., New York, N.Y., c. 1869. [39]

504. Mills and Co., Engravers, Des Moines, Iowa, c. 1876.

505. J. C. Barnes and Co., 96 Main St., Batavia, N.Y., c. 1876. [10]

*506. Southworth and Simpson, Foreign and Domestic Dry Goods, 101 Main St., Batavia,
N.Y., c. 1876. [10]*

507. *Kenyon's Variety Store, 72 Main St., Batavia, N.Y., c. 1876.* [10]

508. *T. T. Brown and Co., 166 Main St., Cincinnati, Ohio, c. 1876. [24]*

509. *E. Myer's and Co., 40 Main St., Cincinnati, Ohio, c. 1876. [24]*

510. *Pioneer Spice and Mustard Mills, 90 W. Second St., Cincinnati, Ohio, c. 1876. [24]*

511. *A. D. Smith and Co. Clock Warehouse, the Gothic Arcade, 184–186 Main St., Cincinnati, Ohio, c. 1876. [24]*

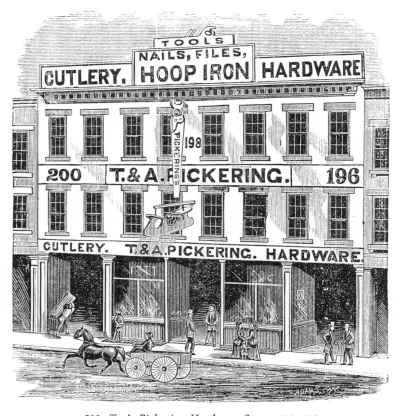

512. *T. A. Pickering Hardware Store, 196, 198–200 Main St., Cincinnati, Ohio, c. 1876. [24]*

513. *Rudolph Wurlitzer and Brother, 115 Main St., Cincinnati, Ohio, c. 1876. [24]*

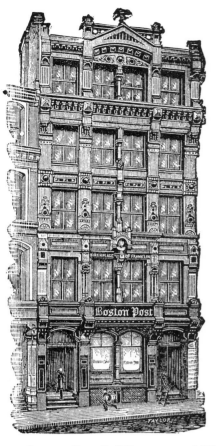

514. Boston Post Building, 15–17 Milk St., Boston, Mass., c. 1879. [25]

515. Banking house of Gilmore, Dunlap and Co., 108–110 W. Fourth St., Cincinnati, Ohio. c. 1876. [24]

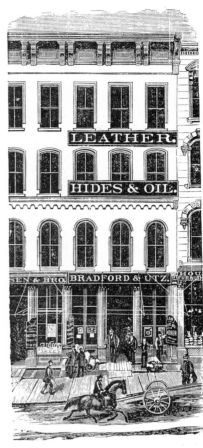

516. Bradford and Utz Leather Salesrooms, 129 Main St., Cincinnati, Ohio, c. 1876. [24]

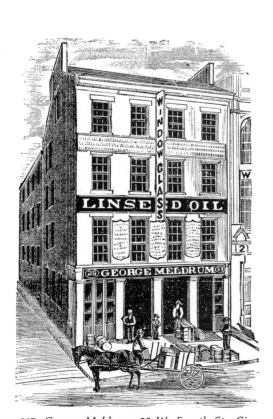

517. George Meldrum, 23 W. Fourth St., Cincinnati, Ohio, c. 1876. [24]

518. John Holland's Gold Pen Manufactory, 19 W. Fourth St., Cincinnati, Ohio, c. 1876. [24]

519. Randall and Aston, Booksellers and Stationers, 109 S. High St., Columbus, Ohio, c. 1873. [42]

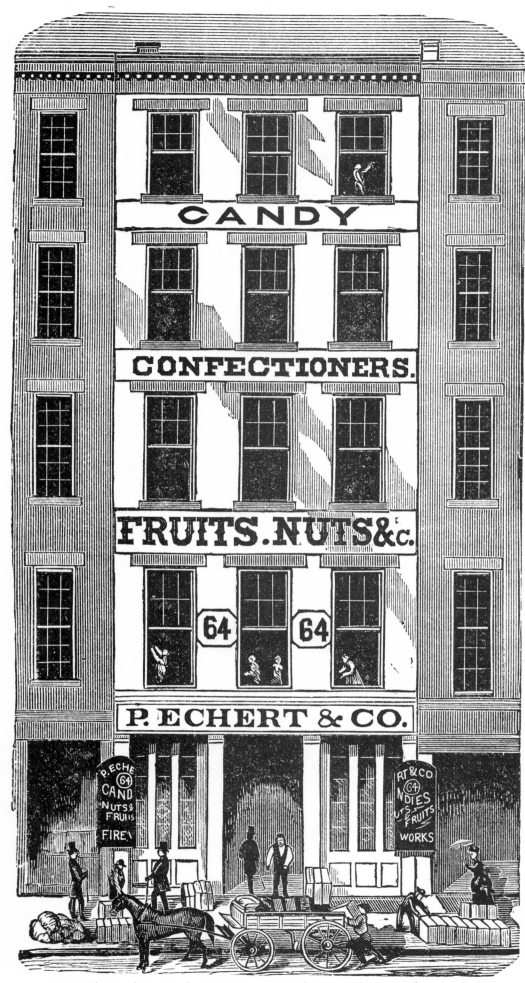

520. *P. Echert and Co., Candy Manufactory, 64 Walnut St., Cincinnati, Ohio, c. 1876.* [24]

G. COPE & CO.
IMPORTERS & JOBBERS OF SILK GOODS

CALEB COPE & CO
IMPORTERS & JOBBERS OF
SILK GOODS
18

Devereux Del et Sc

521. *Cope and Co.'s Dry Goods Bazaar, Market St., Philadelphia, Penn., c. 1854. [15]*

522. Equitable Life-Assurance Society Building, Milk and Devonshire Sts., Boston, Mass., c. 1889. [25]

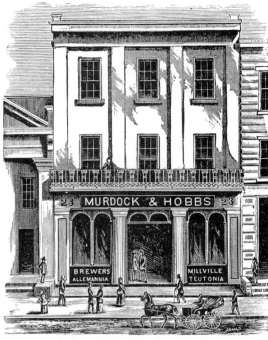

523. Murdock and Hobbs General Underwriters Agency, 23 W. Third St., Cincinnati, Ohio, c. 1876. [24]

524. H. H. May, Druggist, Free and Middle Sts., Portland, Maine, c. 1862. [45]

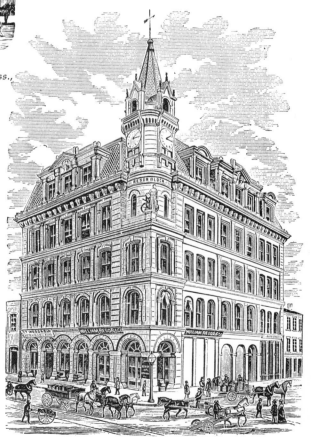

525. William Resor and Co., Stove Manufacturers, Race and Front Sts., Cincinnati, Ohio, c. 1876. [24]

526. John Church and Co., Music Publishers, 66 W. Fourth St., Cincinnati, Ohio, c. 1876. [24]

527. Macullar, Parker and Co., Clothiers, 398–400 Washington St., Boston, Mass., c. 1889. [25]

528. Safe Deposit Co. of Cincinnati, Third St., Cincinnati, Ohio, c. 1876. [24]

529. William G. Bell and Co., Provisions, 48–54 Commercial St., Boston, Mass., c. 1889. [25]

530. Connecticut Mutual Life Insurance Co. Building, Hartford, Conn., c. 1884. [1]

531. *Broadway and Eighteenth St., New York, N.Y., c. 1869.* [39]

532. *Broadway and Leonard St., New York, N.Y., c. 1869.* [39]

533. Dellinger's Opera House, 105–107 Main St., Batavia, N.Y., c. 1876. [10]

534. *Middle St., Portland, Maine, c. 1876. [14]*

535. *R. O. Holden, Dry Goods, Batavia, N.Y. [10]*

536. *Frank Leslie's Publishing House, 53–57 Park Pl., New York, N.Y., c. 1884.* [1]

537. The Van Winkle block, Rutherford, N.J., c. 1876. [43]

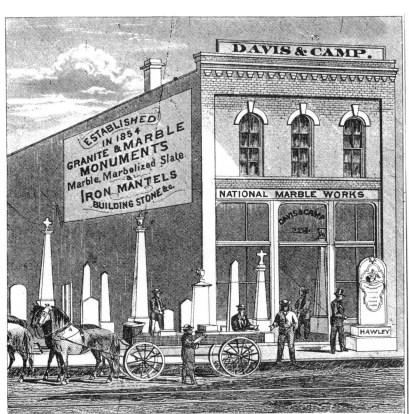

538. Davis and Camp, 224 E. Third St., Davenport, Iowa, c. 1876.

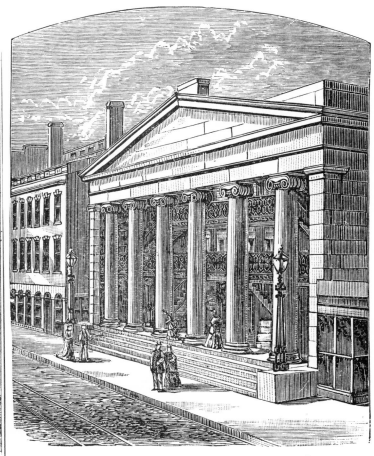

539. The Arcade (built 1828: James Bucklin and Russell Warren, architects), Westminster and Weybosset Sts., Providence, R.I., c. 1886. [16]

540. Broadway and Eleventh St., New York, N.Y., c. 1869. [39]

541. Macullar, Parker and Co., Piece Goods, 112
Westminster St., Providence, R.I., c. 1886. [16]

542. Butler Exchange, Exchange Pl., Providence, R.I., c. 1886. [16]

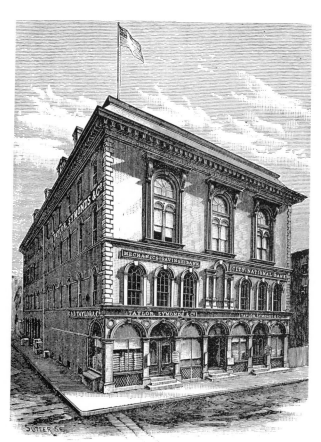

543. Taylor, Symonds and Co., Dry Goods, 76–96
Weybosset St., Providence, R.I., c. 1886. [16]

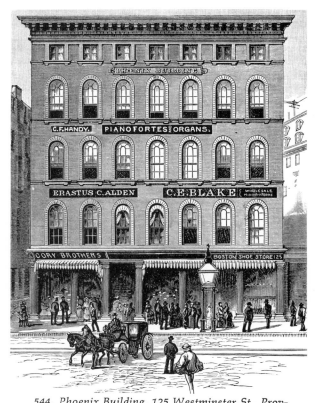

544. Phoenix Building, 125 Westminster St., Providence, R.I., c. 1886. [16]

545. *Cook and Aldrich, Ladies' Furs, Hats and Caps, 147 Washington St., Boston, Mass., c. 1862.* [45]

546. *J. S. Cook and Co., 155 W. Fourth St., Cincinnati, Ohio, c. 1876.* [24]

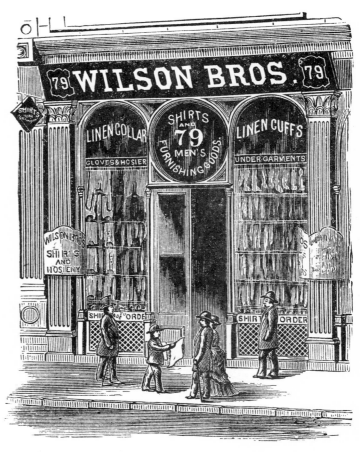

547. *Wilson Bros., Shirt Manufacturers, 79 W. Fourth St., Cincinnati, Ohio, c. 1876* [24]

548. *Duhme and Co., Jewelers, Fourth and Walnut Sts., Cincinnati, Ohio, c. 1876.* [24]

549. *John Shillito and Co., Dry Goods, W. Fourth St., Cincinnati, Ohio, c. 1876.* [24]

550. *Horticultural Hall, Broad St., Philadelphia, Penn., c. 1876.*
[26]

551. *Academy of Music, Broad and Locust Sts., Philadelphia,*
Penn., c. 1876. [26]

552. *Bowery Theatre, Bowery and Canal Sts., New York, N.Y.,*
c. 1845.

553. *Walnut Street Theatre, Walnut and Ninth Sts., Philadelphia, Penn.*

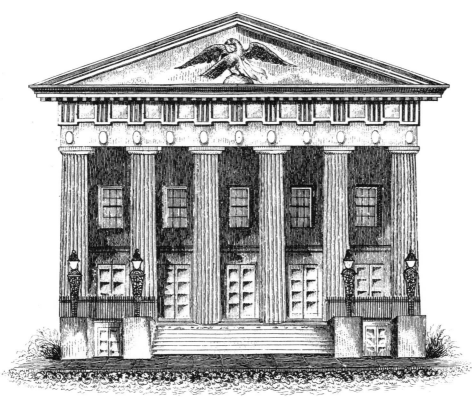

554. *Old Bowery Theatre (erected 1825; Ithiel Town, architect),*
Bowery and Canal Sts., New York, N.Y., c. 1833.

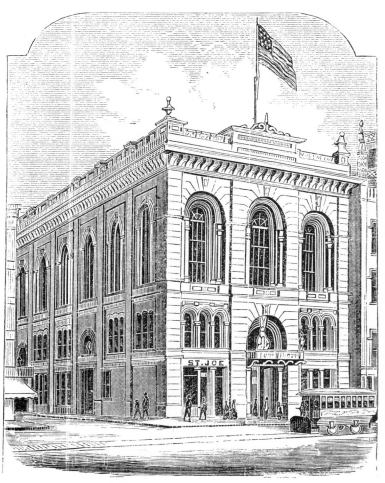

555. Grand Opera House, Vine and Longworth Sts., Cincinnati, Ohio, c. 1876. [24]

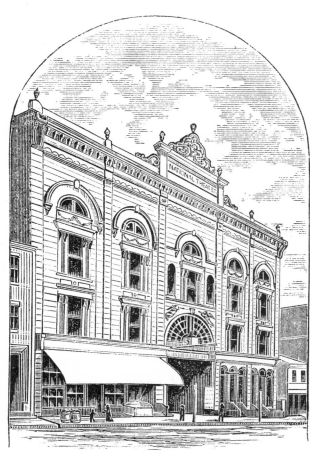

556. National Theatre (opened c. 1850), Sycamore St., Cincinnati, Ohio, c. 1876. [24]

557. Wood's Theatre, Vine and Sixth Sts., Cincinnati, Ohio, c. 1876. [24]

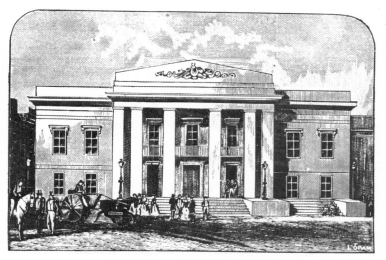

558. Italian Opera House, New York, N. Y.

559. *Ford's Theatre, Tenth St., Washington, D.C., c. 1886.* [30]

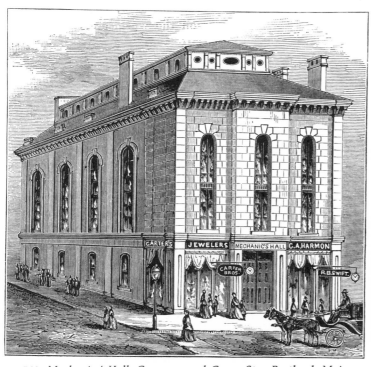

560. *Mechanics' Hall, Congress and Casco Sts., Portland, Maine,
c. 1876.* [14]

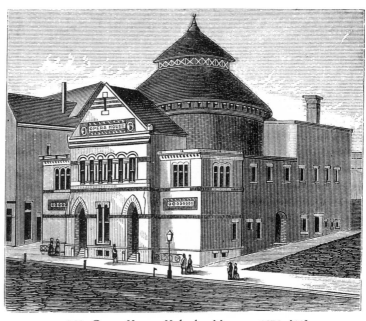

561. *Opera House, Holyoke, Mass., c. 1879.* [18]

562. The Hippodrome (built 1853; demolished 1856), Madison Sq., New York, N.Y., c. 1853.
[15]

563. The Hippodrome, c. 1853. [15]

564. *Interior, Niblo's Garden Opera House (erected 1849), Broadway and Prince St., New York, N.Y., c. 1853.* [15]

565. *Entrance Hall, Niblo's Garden Opera House, c. 1853.* [15]

566. *Ballroom, Niblo's Garden Opera House, c. 1853.* [15]

567. *Horticultural Hall (dedicated 1865), Tremont St., Boston, Mass., c. 1889.* [25]

568. *Tremont Temple (built 1880), Tremont St., Boston, Mass., c. 1889* [25]

569. *Gymnasium, Fourth St., Cincinnati, Ohio, c. 1876.* [24]

570. *A Bowery dime museum, New York, N.Y., c. 1891.* [7]

571. United States Government Building, Centennial Exhibition, Fairmont Park, Philadelphia, Penn., 1876. [26]

572. Women's Pavilion, Centennial Exhibition, Fairmont Park, Philadelphia, Penn., 1876. [26]

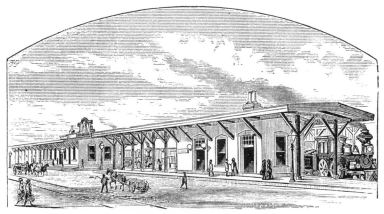

573. Ohio and Mississippi Depot (erected 1873), W. Front and
Mill Sts., Cincinnati, Ohio, c. 1876. [24]

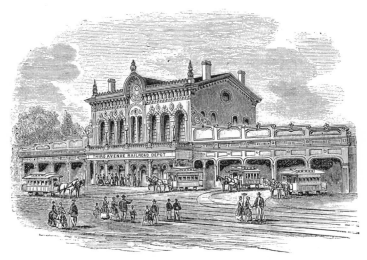

·574. Third Avenue Railroad Depot, New York, N.Y., c. 1869. [39]

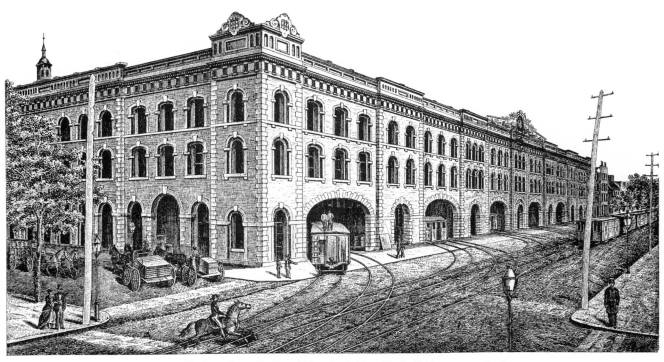

575. Hudson River Railroad Terminal, New York, N.Y., c. 1869. [39]

576. *Concord Railroad Depot, Concord, N.H.*

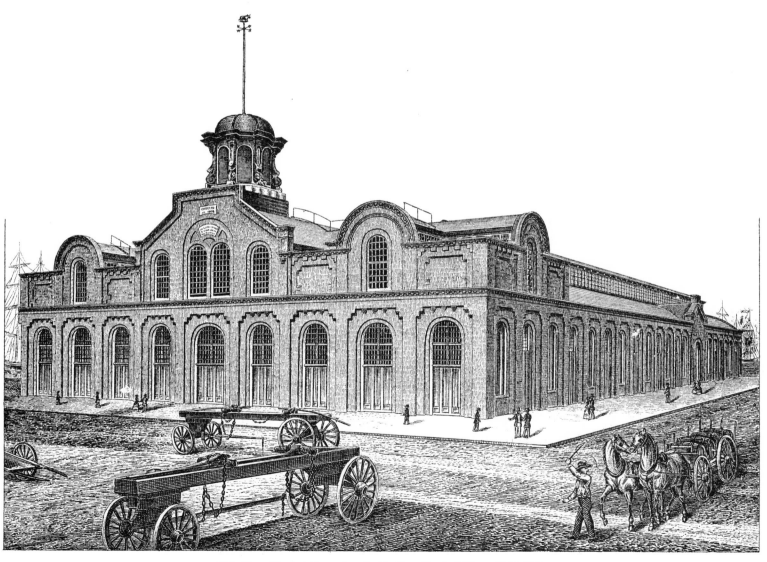

577. *New Market, Seventeenth St., New York, N.Y., c. 1869.* [39]

578. *Calvert Railroad Station, Calvert St., Baltimore, Md., c. 1853.* [15]

579. *Centennial Depot of the Philadelphia and Reading Railroad, Fairmont Park, Philadelphia, Penn., 1876.* [26]

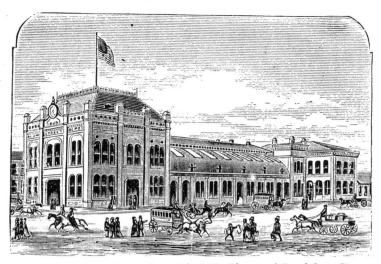

580. Plum Street Depot (erected 1863), Plum and Pearl Sts., Cincinnati, Ohio, c. 1876. [24]

581. Little Miami Railroad Depot (erected 1851), Kilgore and Front Sts., Cincinnati, Ohio, c. 1876. [24]

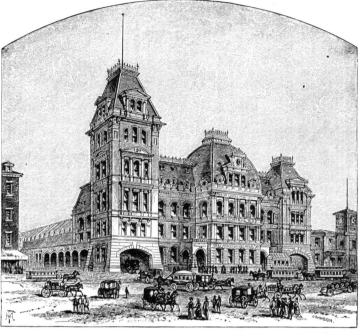

582. Station of the Boston and Maine Railroad (built 1871), Causeway and Nashua Sts., Boston, Mass., c. 1889. [25]

583. Old Colony Railroad Depot, Kneeland and South Sts., Boston, Mass., c. 1889. [25]

584. Station of the Providence Division of the Old Colony Railroad, Park Sq., Boston, Mass., c. 1889. [25]

585. Block signal station on the Pennsylvania Railroad, c. 1876. [26]

586. The Exchange (erected 1771: William Rigby Naylor, architect), Charleston, S.C., c. 1828.

*587. U. S. Branch Bank (erected 1822: Martin Thompson, architect; now the south facade
of the American Wing of the Metropolitan Museum of Art), Wall St., New York, N.Y.*

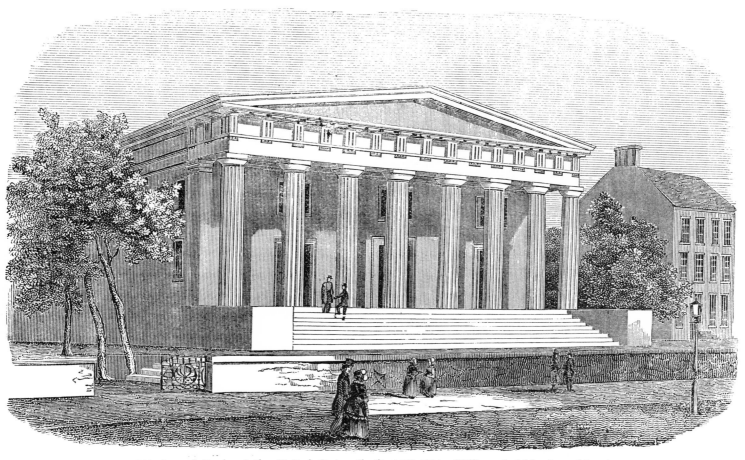

588. *Second Bank of the United States (built 1818-1824: William Strickland, architect), Philadelphia, Penn., c. 1848. [38]*

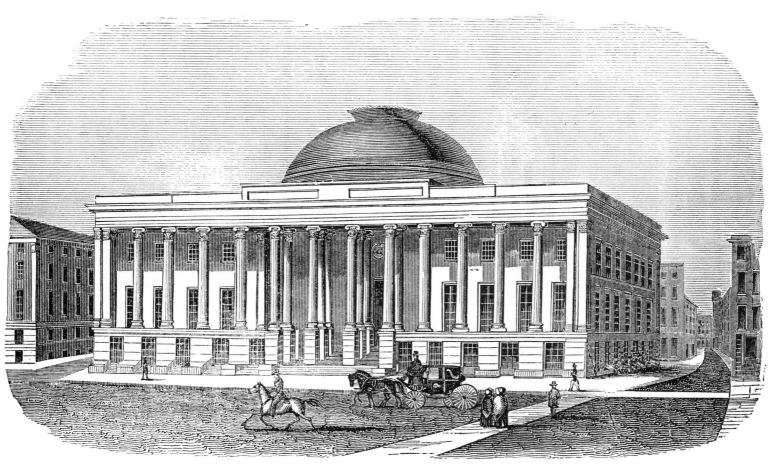

589. *Third Merchants' Exchange (built 1842: Isiah Rogers, architect), 55 Wall St., New York, N.Y., c. 1848. [38]*

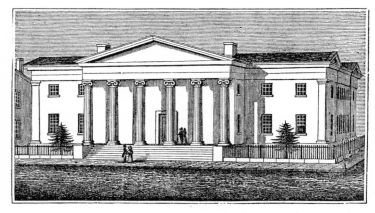

590. *Union Bank and the National Bank, Wall St., New York, N.Y.*

591. *United States Mint (built 1830: William Strickland, architect), Chestnut and Centre Sts., Philadelphia, Penn., c. 1843.* [12]

592. *Suffolk Bank (erected 1834: Isiah Rogers, architect), State St., Boston, Mass.*

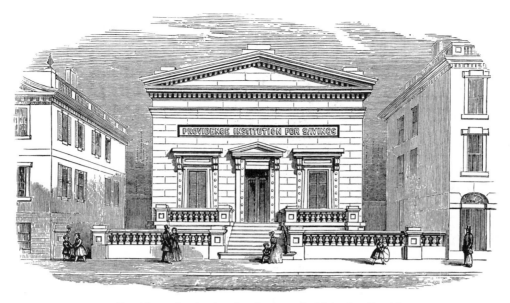

593. *Providence Institution for Savings, S. Main St., Providence,
R.I., c. 1886.* [16]

594. *Bank Building, Hackensack, N.J., c. 1876.* [43]

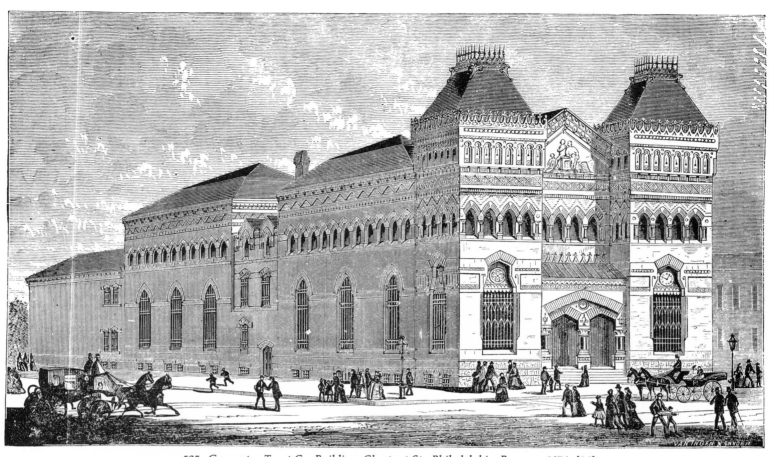

595. *Guarantee Trust Co. Building, Chestnut St., Philadelphia, Penn., c. 1876.* [26]

596. *New York Seamen's Exchange Building, Cherry St., New York, N.Y., c. 1871.* [17]

597. *Provident Life and Trust Co., Chestnut St., Philadelphia, Penn., c. 1876.* [26]

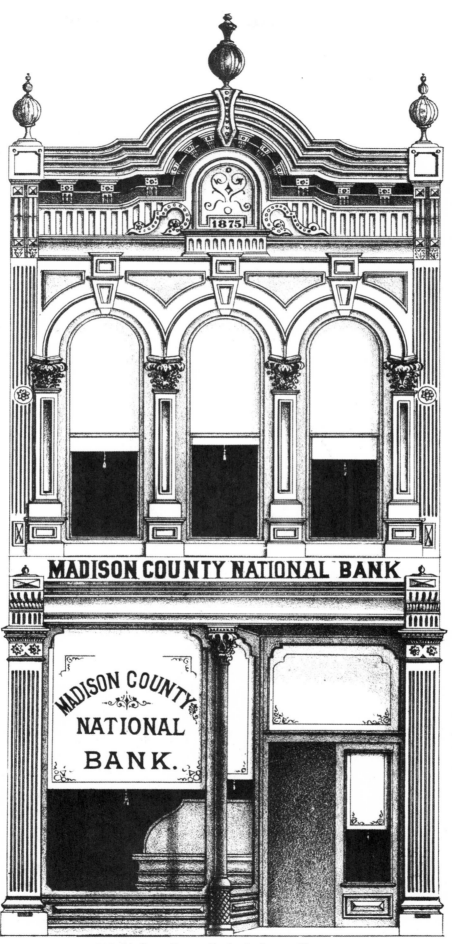

598. *Madison County Bank, Anderson, Ill., c. 1875.*

599. Almshouse (built 1801; demolished 1825), Leveret St., Boston, Mass. [41]

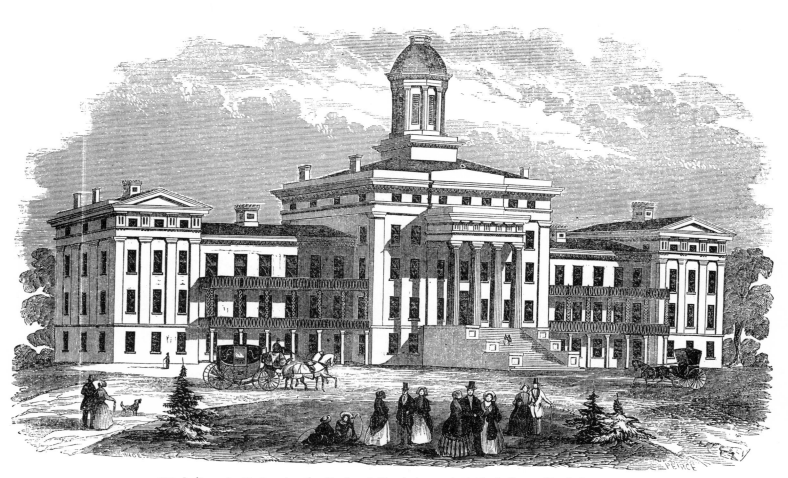

600. Indiana Institution for the Deaf and Dumb (opened 1844), Indianapolis, Ind., c. 1854.
[15]

601. Ohio Blind Institution, Columbus, Ohio, c. 1847. [22]

602. Ohio Deaf and Dumb Asylum, Columbus, Ohio, c. 1847. [22]

603. Orphan Asylum, Norfolk, Va.

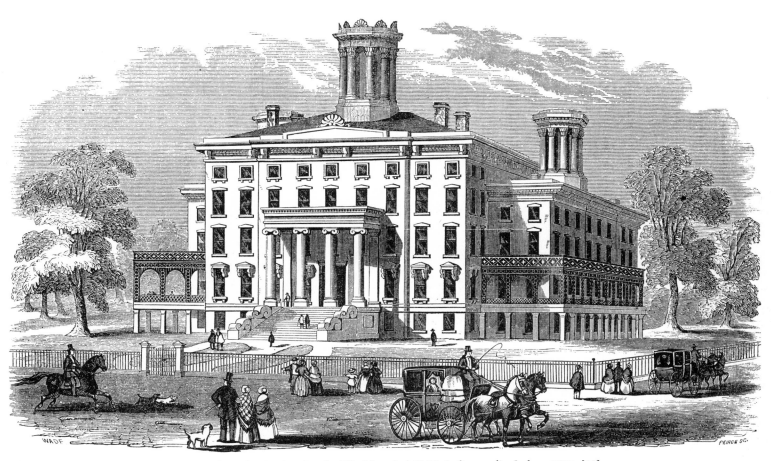

604. Indiana Institution for the Blind (erected 1847), Indianapolis, Ind., c. 1854. [15]

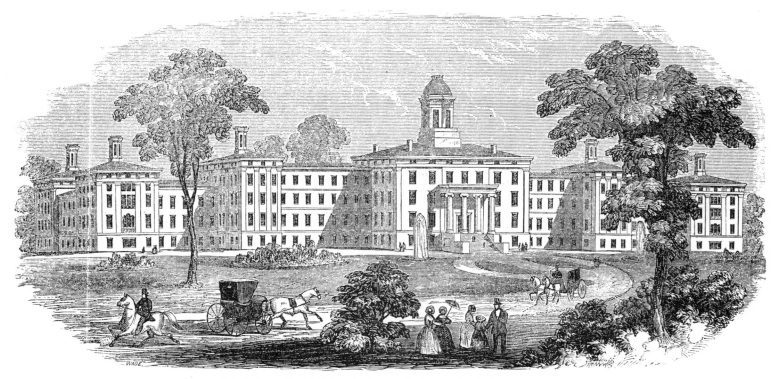

605. Indiana Hospital for the Insane, Indianapolis, Ind., c. 1854. [15]

606. Boston City Hospital (dedicated 1864), Harrison Ave., Boston, Mass., c. 1889. [25]

607. *Pennsylvania Hospital (Eighth St. wing erected 1755: Samuel Rhoads, architect), Spruce & Eighth Sts., Philadelphia, Penn., c. 1843.* [12]

608. *U. S. Naval Asylum (erected 1835: William Strickland, architect,) Philadelphia, Penn., c. 1843.* [12]

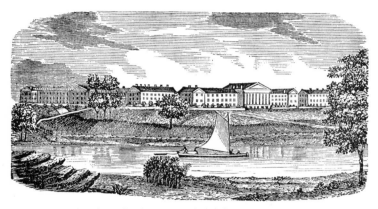

609. *Blockley Almshouse, Philadelphia, Penn., c. 1843.* [12]

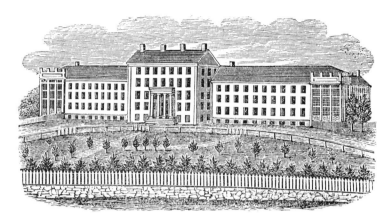

610. *State Lunatic Hospital (erected 1831), Worcester, Mass., c. 1839.* [3]

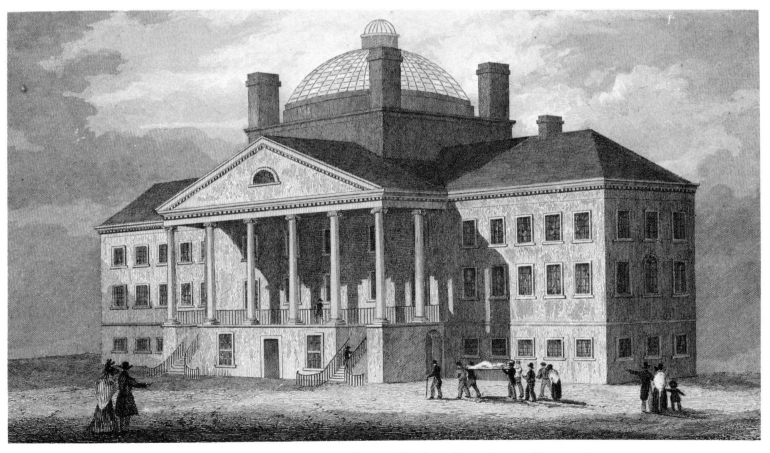

611. *General Hospital (erected 1818: Charles Bulfinch, architect), Boston, Mass., c. 1831.*

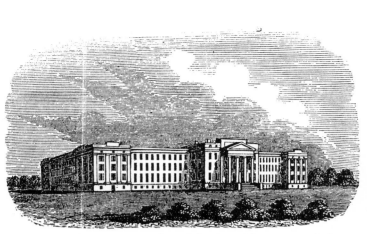

612. *Ohio Lunatic Asylum, Columbus, Ohio, c. 1847.* [22]

613. *Roman Catholic Home for Orphans, Harrison Ave., Boston, Mass., c. 1889.* [25]

614. *New Hospital for Lunatics (work in progress 1873: Levi F. Schofield, architect), Columbus, Ohio.* [42]

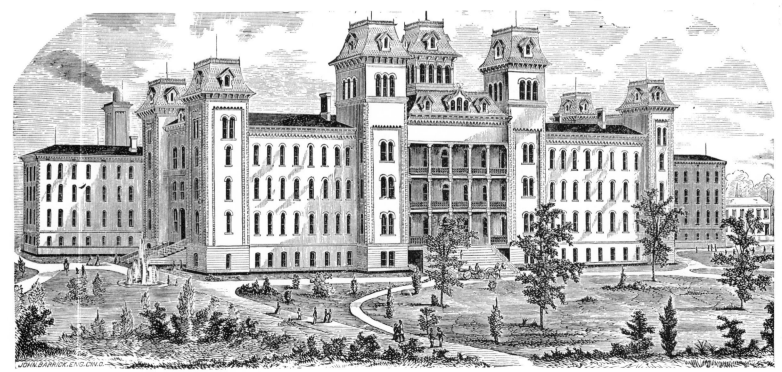

615. *Ohio Institution for the Deaf and Dumb (erected 1868: J. M. Blackburn, architect), Columbus, Ohio, c. 1873.* [42]

616. Mount Sinai Hospital, Lexington Ave. and E. Sixty-sixth
St., New York, N.Y., c. 1885. [11]

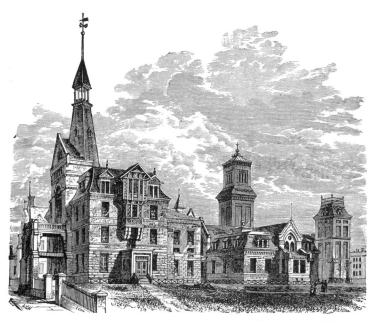

617. Roosevelt Hospital, W. Fifty-ninth St., New York, N.Y., c.
1885. [11]

618. New York Hospital, Fifteenth St., New York, N.Y., c. 1885.
[11]

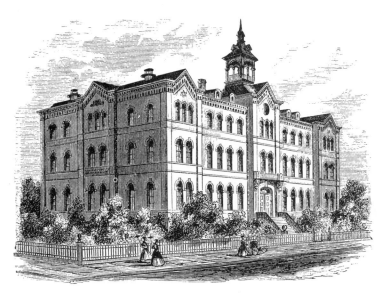

619. Hebrew Benevolent and Orphan Asylum Society, E. Seventy-
seventh St., New York, N.Y., c. 1869. [39]

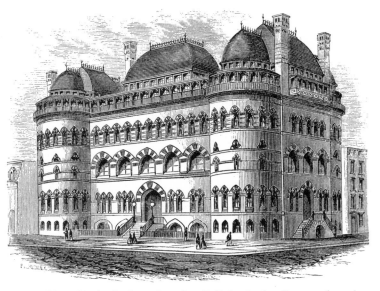

620. New York Society for the Relief of the Ruptured and
Crippled, Lexington Ave. and E. Forty-second St., New York,
N.Y., c. 1869. [39]

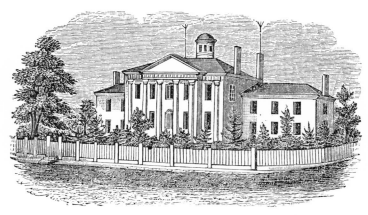

621. *Redwood Library (erected 1748: Peter Harrison, architect),*
Newport, R.I., c. 1875. [13]

622. *Antiquarian Hall (library, erected 1820), Worcester, Mass.,*
c. 1839. [3]

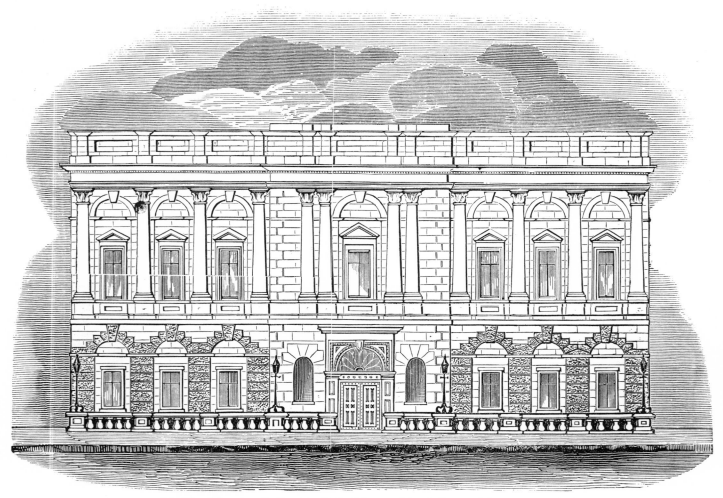

623. *The Atheneum (built 1845: E. C. Cabot, architect), Boston, Mass., c. 1849. [35]*

624. Interior, Astor Library (built 1849: Griffith Thomas, architect), 425 Lafayette St., New York, N.Y., c. 1854. [15]

625. Astor Library, c. 1854. [15]

626. Rogers Free Library Building, Bristol, R.I., c. 1886. [16]

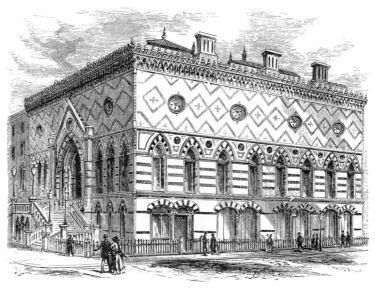

627. *National Academy of Design, Fourth Ave. and Twenty-third St., New York, N. Y., c. 1869.* [39]

628. *Boston Museum of Fine Arts (first section completed 1876: original design by Sturgis and Brigham, architects), Dartmouth St. and St. James Ave., Boston, Mass.* [25]

629. *New Jersey State Building, Centennial Exhibition, Fairmount Park, Philadelphia, Penn., 1876.* [26]

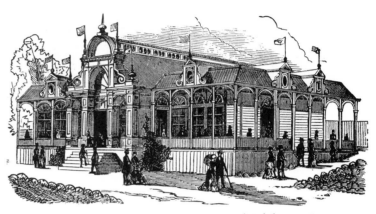

630. *Philadelphia City Building, Centennial Exhibition, Fairmount Park, Philadelphia, Penn., 1876.* [26]

631. *Colorado and Kansas State Building, Centennial Exhibition, Fairmount Park, Philadelphia, Penn., 1876.* [26]

632. *Michigan State Building, Centennial Exhibition, Fairmount Park, Philadelphia, Penn., 1876.* [26]

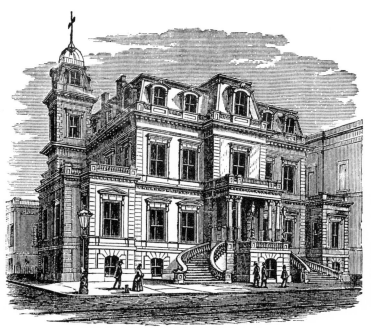

633. *Union League, Broad St., Philadelphia, Penn., c. 1876.* [27]

634. *Masonic Temple, Broad St., Philadelphia, Penn., c. 1876.* [27]

635. *Masonic Temple, Chestnut St., Philadelphia, Penn., c. 1876.*
[26]

636. *Masonic Hall, Broadway, New York, N.Y., c.*
1839. [29]

637. Masonic Temple (dedicated 1867), Tremont and Boyleston Sts., Boston, Mass., c. 1895.

[32]

638. *Green Dragon Tavern, Union St., Boston, Mass., c. 1770.* [41]

639. *Lamb Tavern, Washington St., Boston, Mass.* [41]

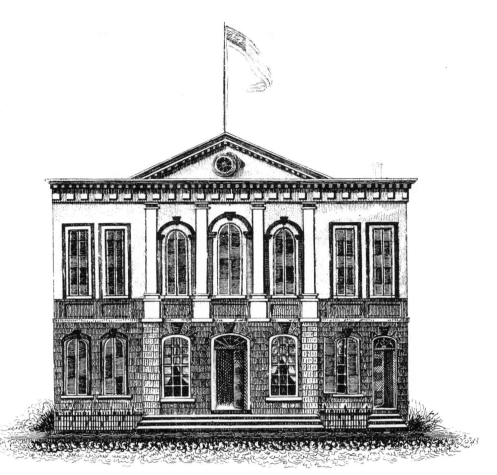

640. *Washington Hotel, Broadway, New York, N.Y., c. 1833.*

641. *Exchange Coffee House (built 1808; demolished 1853), Congress Sq., Boston, Mass., c. 1825.* [41]

642. *Passaic Hotel, Bank and River Sts., Paterson, N.J., c. 1868.*
[2]

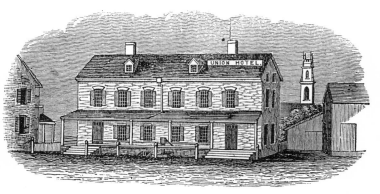

643. *Union Hotel (erected 1781), Hope, N.J., c. 1868.* [2]

644. *Thayer's Hotel, Littleton, N.H., c. 1884.* [1]

645. *Pavilion Hotel, Rochester, Penn., c. 1884.* [1]

646. *Stevens House Hotel, Canaan, Conn., c. 1884.* [1]

647. *Joslin House Hotel, Webster, Mass., c. 1884.* [1]

648. *Westfield House Hotel, Westfield, N.Y., c. 1884. [1]*

649. *Prospect House Hotel, Waltham, Mass., c. 1884 [1]*

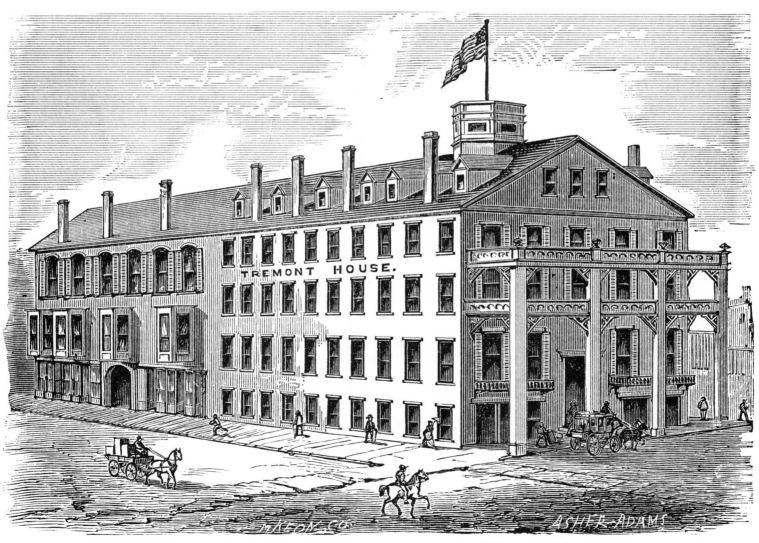

650. *Tremont House Hotel, Main and Pearl Sts., Nashua, N.H., c. 1884. [1]*

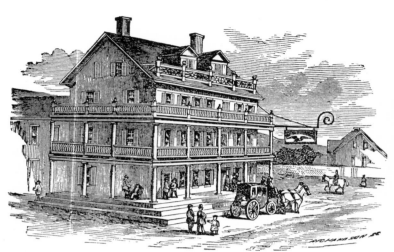

651. *Stoddard House Hotel, Broadway, Farmington, Maine, c. 1862. [45]*

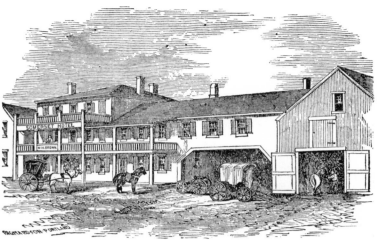

652. *Somerset Hotel, Anson, Maine, c. 1862. [45]*

653. *Mansion House Hotel, Greenfield, Mass., c. 1879. [18]*

654. Parry House Hotel, Highland Falls, N.Y., c. 1875. [5]

655. American House Hotel, Schaghticoke, N.Y., c. 1884. [1]

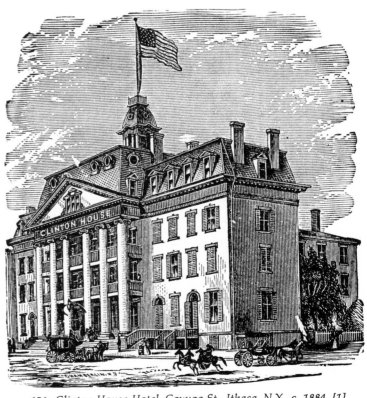

656. Clinton House Hotel, Cayuga St., Ithaca, N.Y., c. 1884. [1]

657. Ottawa House Hotel (built 1853), Cushing's Island, Portland, Maine, c. 1876. [14]

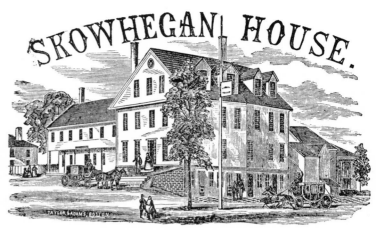

658. Skowhegan House Hotel, Elm and Madison Sts., Skowhegan, Maine, c. 1862. [45]

659. National Hotel, Warwick, N.Y., c. 1875. [5]

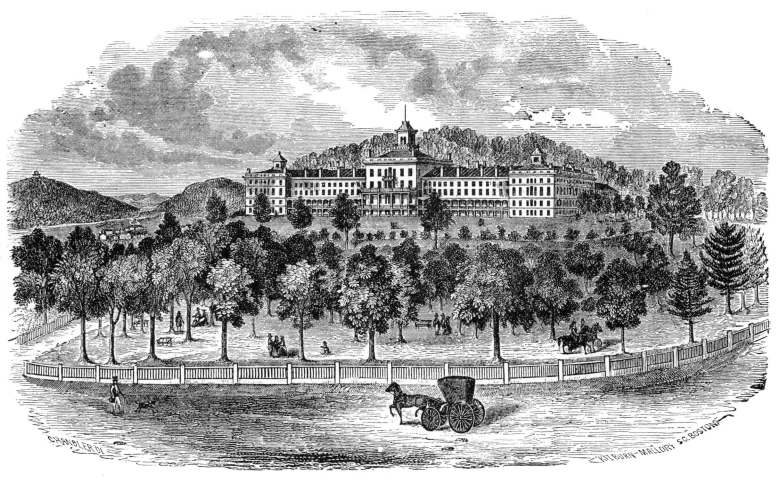

660. *Round Hill Hotel, Northampton, Mass., c. 1874.* [28]

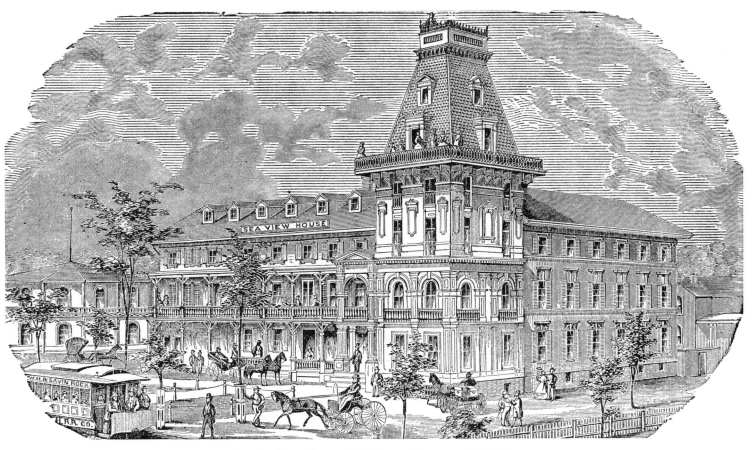

661. *Sea View House, West Haven, Conn., c. 1874.* [28]

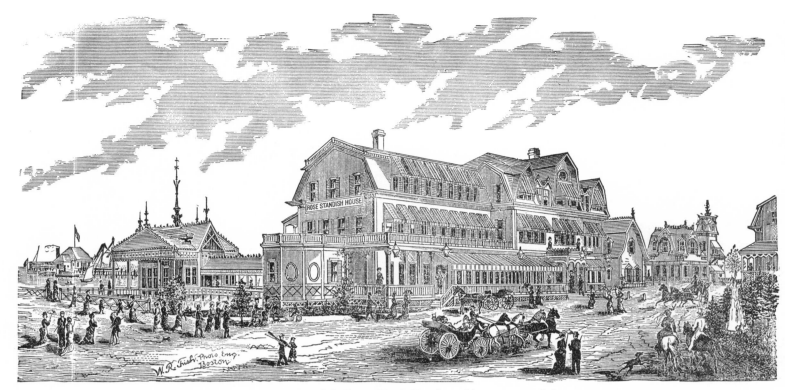

662. *Rose Standish House Hotel, Hingham, Mass., c. 1884. [1]*

663. *Grand Union Hotel (built c. 1871), Park Ave. and Forty-second St., New York, N.Y., c. 1884. [1]*

664. *Greylock Hall Hotel, Williamstown, Mass., c. 1884. [1]*

665. *Burnet House Hotel (erected 1849), Third and Vine Sts.,*
Cincinnati, Ohio, c. 1876. [24]

666. *Charleston Hotel, Charleston, S.C., c. 1884. [1]*

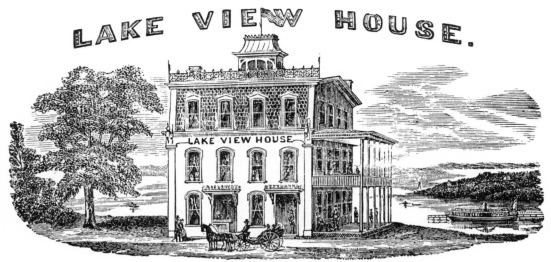

667. *Lakeview House Hotel, Skaneateles, N.Y., c. 1884.* [1]

668. *Hill's Mansion House Hotel, East Hampton, Mass., c. 1884.*
[1]

669. *Cowles' Hotel, North Manchester, Mass., c. 1884.* [1]

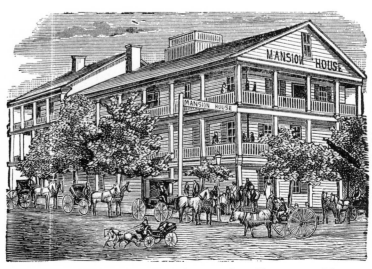

670. *Mansion House Hotel, Fernandina, Fla., c. 1884.* [1]

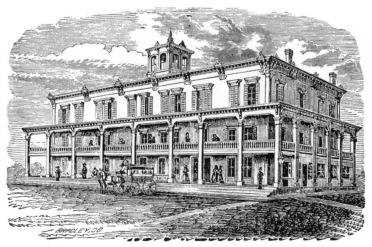

671. *Stevens House Hotel, Vergennes, Vt., c. 1884.* [1]

672. *Cumberland House Hotel, Plattsburgh, N.Y., c. 1884.* [1]

673. *The Henrie House Hotel, Third St., Cincinnati, Ohio, c. 1876.* [24]

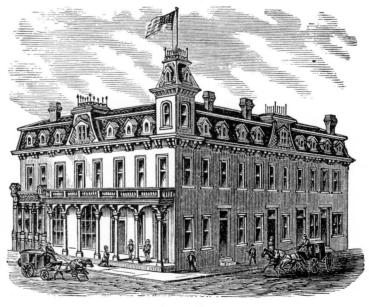

674. *Newton's Hotel, Woodbury, N.J., c. 1884.* [1]

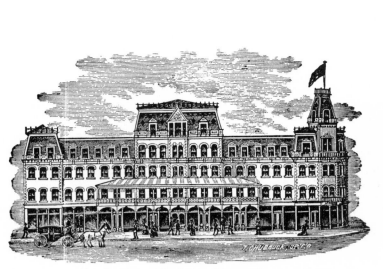

675. *Brooks House Hotel, Brattleboro, Vt., c. 1884.* [1]

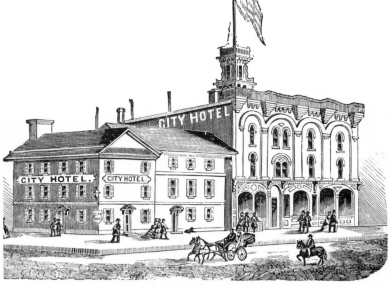

676. *City Hotel, Chester, Penn., c. 1884.* [1]

677. *Florence House Hotel, Fourth Ave. and Eighteenth St., New York, N.Y., c. 1884.* [1]

678. *St. James' Hotel, Wheeling, W. Va., c. 1884.* [1]

679. *Grand Hotel (built 1874), Central Ave. and Fourth St., Cincinnati, Ohio, c. 1876.* [24]

680. *Hotel Vendome, Commonwealth Ave. and Dartmouth St., Boston, Mass., c. 1889.* [25]

681. Hotel Brunswick (built 1874: Peabody & Stearns, architects), Boyleston and Clarendon
Sts., Boston, Mass., c. 1889. [25]

682. Hotel, Fairmount, N.J., c. 1876. [43]

683. Sturdevant & Benedicts Wool Hat Manufactory, Danbury, Conn.

684. Granite Mill (built c. 1853), Burrillville, R.I., c. 1878. [20]

685. Rumford Chemical Works, S. Water St., Providence, R.I., c. 1886. [16]

686. Slater Mill (built 1793), Pawtucket, R.I., c. 1886. [16]

687. Glendale Mills (built c. 1853), Burrillville, R.I., c. 1878. [20]

688. Manufactories, Seneca Falls, N.Y., c. 1876. [19]

689. A. B. Jones, Coal, Rutherford, N.J., c. 1876. [43]

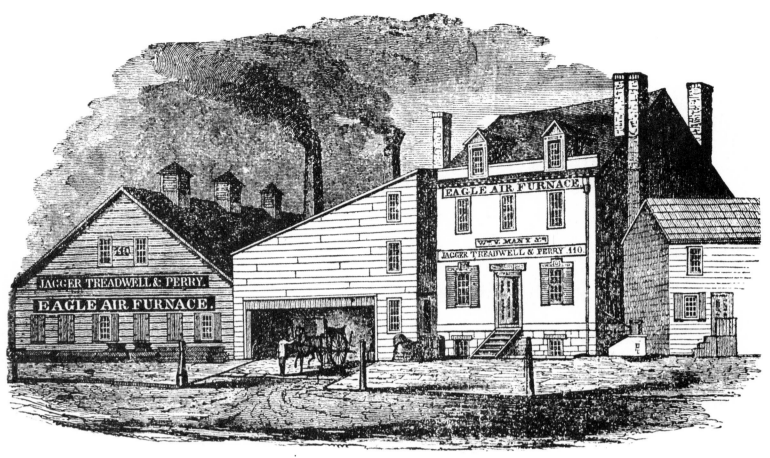

690. *Jagger, Treadwell & Perry, Pot Manufactory, Albany, N.Y.*

691. *Rathbun Merchant & Custom Mills, East Pembroke, N.Y., c. 1876.* [10]

692. Collignon Bros., Manufacturers of Patent Folding Chairs, Cloister, N.J., c. 1876. [43]

693. *Manufactory of the Tornado Windmill Co., Elba, N.Y., c. 1876.* [10]

694. Manufacturing establishments, Paterson, N.J., c. 1868. [2]

695. Ashland Furnace and Coal Works, Ashland, Ky., c. 1876. [24]

696. DeBaun's Carriage Factory, Union St., Hackensack, N.J., c. 1876. [43]

697. *Site of the Revolutionary War foundry, Salisbury, Conn., c. 1854.* [15]

698. *Harrisville Woolen Mills, Harrisville, R.I., c. 1878.* [20]

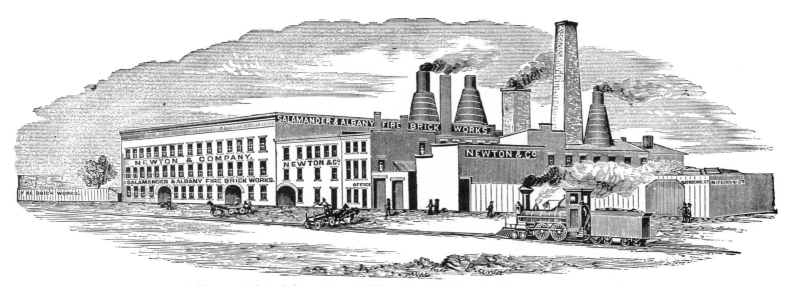

699. *Newton & Co.'s Salamander and Albany Fire Brick Works, Albany, N.Y., c. 1884.* [1]

700. *John L. Foster's Carriage Factory, 1–5 State St., Batavia, N.Y., c. 1876.* [10]

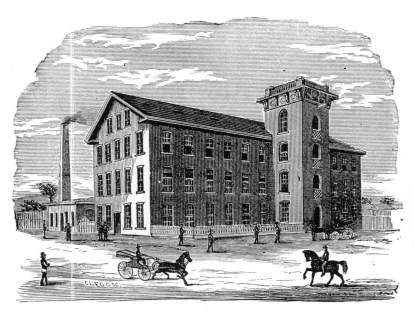

701. *Belding Bros. & Co. Silk Mills, Rockville, Conn., c. 1876.* [24]

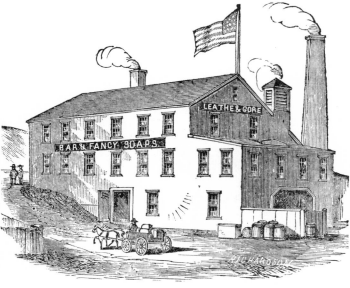

702. *Leathe & Gore, Fancy Soap Manufacturers, Summer and Canal Sts., Portland, Maine, c. 1862.* [45]

704. *Mehrhof Brick Manufacturers, Little Ferry, N.J., c. 1876.* [43]

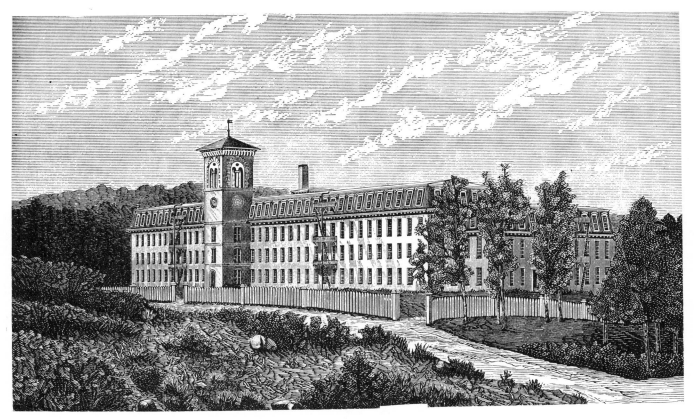

703. *Mill at Manchaug, Sutton, Mass., c. 1878.* [6]

705. Kalamazoo Iron Works, Kalamazoo, Mich., c. 1884. [1]

706. *J. P. Hale, Piano Manufactory, Tenth Ave. and Thirty-fifth St., New York, N.Y., c.*
1884. [1]

707. *James Cunningham & Son, Carriage Manufactory (Harvey Ellis, architect), Rochester,*
N.Y., c. 1884. [1]

708. *C. Magnus, Eagle Brewery, Cedar Rapids, Iowa, c. 1876.*

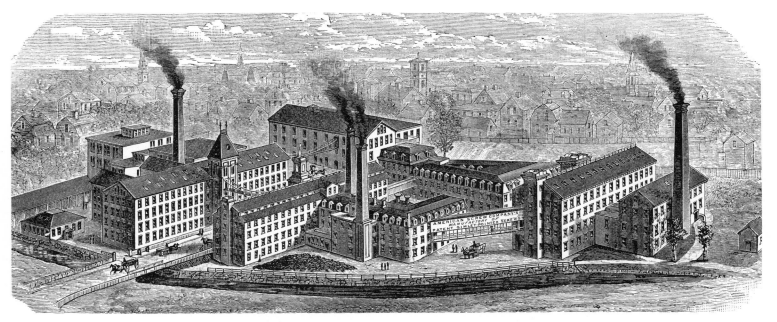

709. *American Screw Co. Mills, Providence, R.I., c. 1886. [16]*

710. *Kensington Fire Brick Works, Philadelphia, Penn., c. 1884. [1]*

711. *Greenwood Iron Works, Orange County, N.Y., c. 1875.* [5]

RON WORKS.
CO. N.Y.
RROTT.

712. *South Boston Iron Co., South Boston, Mass., c. 1884.* [1]

713. Minett & Co. Varnish Works, Passaic, N.J., c. 1884 [1]

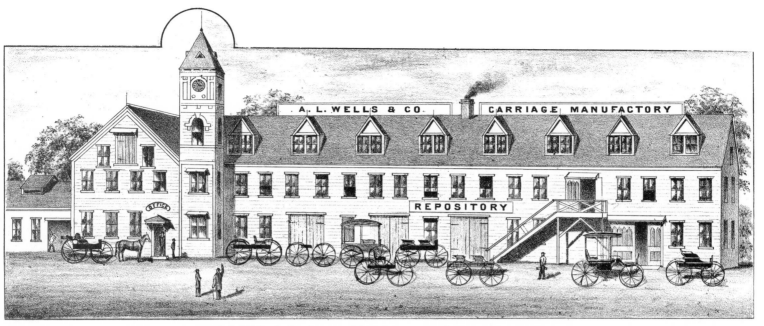

714. *A. L. Wells & Co. Carriage Manufactory, Hopkintown, R.I., c. 1878.* [20]

715. *John Schaefer's Western Brewery, Muscatine, Iowa, c. 1876.*

716. *Wheeler & Wilson Manufacturing Co., Bridgeport, Conn., c. 1876.*

Worley & Bracher Lith. 320 Chestnut St. Philad.ᵃ

717. *Metropolitan Fire Department Headquarters, 127 Mercer St., New York, N.Y., c. 1869.* [30]

718. *Gay Street Engine House, Columbus, Ohio, c. 1873.* [42]

719. *South High Street Engine House, Columbus, Ohio, c. 1873.* [42]

720. H. E. & J. Taylor's Stables, Englewood, N.J., c. 1876. [43]

721. Redoubt (built 1764), Penn and Point Sts., Pittsburgh, Penn., c. 1843. [12]

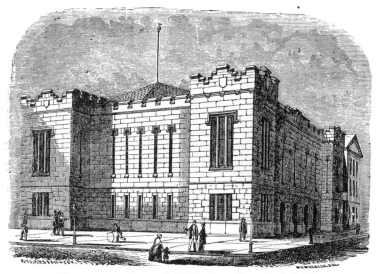

722. City Armory, Elm and White Sts., New York, N.Y., c. 1885. [11]

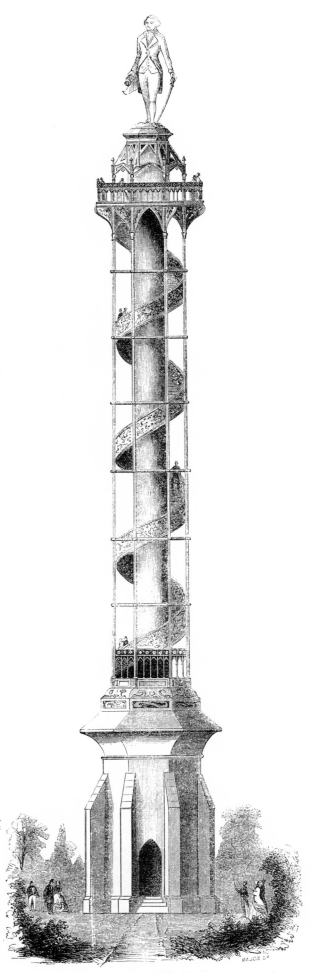

724. *Observatory (built 1807), Congress St., Portland, Maine, c. 1876.* [14]

725. *Washington Monument (built 1815: Robert Mills, architect), Baltimore, Md., c. 1848.* [38]

723. *Standpipe of the Philadelphia Waterworks (proposed design 1853: Birkinbine and Trotter, architects).* [15]

726. *Bemis Heights Monument, Saratoga National Historical Park, Stillwater, N.Y., c. 1893.* [9]

727. *Jefferson Market and fire tower, Sixth Ave. and W. Tenth St., New York, N.Y., c. 1830.* [11]

728. *Observatory, Chelsea, Mass., c. 1854.* [15]

729. *Fox Point observatory, Providence, R.I., c. 1886.* [16]

730. Two-lights (built 1874), Cape Elizabeth, Maine, c. 1876. [14]

731. Whale's-back Light, Isles of Shoals, N.H., c. 1875. [13]

732. Lighthouse & covered way, White Island, N.H., c. 1875. [13]

733. Minot's-ledge Lighthouse, Cohasset, Mass., c. 1874. [31]

734. *White Island Light, N.H., c. 1875.* [13]

735. *New London Light, Conn., c. 1875.* [13]

736. *Portland Light (built 1791), Maine, c. 1876.* [14]

737. *Miles Standish Monument (work in progress 1874), Duxbury, Mass.* [31]

738. *Thatcher's Island Light and fog signals, Cape Ann, Mass., c. 1875.* [13]

739. The mills of East Hampton, Long Island, N.Y., c. 1826. [37]

740. *Windmill, Nantucket, Mass., c. 1875.* [13]

741. *Rhode Island windmill, c. 1875.* [13]

742. *Windmill, Newport, R.I., c. 1848.* [38]

Bibliography

Most of the illustrations used in this book were extracted from the works listed in this Bibliography. The entry for each book listed here is preceded by a number; this number appears as the last element in the captions for the illustrations taken from that book.

The sources of some of the illustrations are unknown. In these cases, no bibliography number appears in the caption.

[1] Asher and Adams, *New Columbian Railroad Atlas and Pictorial Album of American Industry*. New York: George H. Adams and Sons, 1884.

[2] Barber, John Warner, *Historical Collections of New Jersey*. New Haven: John W. Barber, 1868.

[3] ———, *Massachusetts Historical Collections*. Worcester: Dorr, Howland and Co., 1839.

[4] Barnard, Henry, *School Architecture*. New York: A. S. Barnes and Co., 1848.

[5] Beers, F. W., *County Atlas of Orange, New York*. Chicago: Andreas, Baskin and Burr, 1875.

[6] Benedict, Rev. William A., and Tracy, Rev. Hiram A., *History of the Town of Sutton, Massachusetts*. Worcester: Sanford and Co., 1878.

[7] Campbell, Helen, and others, *Darkness and Daylight: Lights and Shadows of New York Life*. Hartford: A. D. Worthington and Co., 1891.

[8] *The Century Magazine*, December, 1886.

[9] Cleaveland, George A., and Campbell, Robert E., *American Landmarks*. Boston: Balch Brothers, 1893.

[10] *Combination Atlas Map of Genesee County, New York*. Philadelphia: Everts, Ensign and Everts, 1876.

[11] Costello, Augustine E., *Our Police Protectors*. New York: Augustine E. Costello, 1885.

[12] Day, Sherman, *Historical Collections of the State of Pennsylvania*. Philadelphia: George W. Gorton, 1843.

[13] Drake, Samuel Adams, *Nooks and Corners of the New England Coast*. New York: Harper and Brothers, 1875.

[14] Elwell, Edward H., *Portland and Vicinity*. Portland: Loring, Short and Harmon, and W. S. Jones, 1876.

[15] *Gleason's Pictorial Drawing-room Companion* Vols. IV-VII. Boston: F. Gleason, 1853-1855.

[16] Greene, Welcome Arnold, *The Providence Plantations for Two Hundred and Fifty Years*. Providence: J. A. and R. A. Reid, 1886.

[17] *Harper's Weekly*, October 21, 1871.

[18] *History of the Connecticut Valley in Massachusetts*, Vol. II. Philadelphia: Louis H. Everts, 1879.

[19] *History of Seneca County, New York*. Philadelphia: Everts, Ensign and Everts, 1876.

[20] *History of the State of Rhode Island*. Philadelphia: Hoag, Wade and Co., 1878.

[21] Hobbs, Clarence W., *Lynn and Surroundings*. Lynn: Lewis and Winship, 1886.

[22] Howe, Henry, *Historical Collections of Ohio*. Cincinnati: Derby Bradley and Co., 1847.

[23] *Illustrated Annual Register of Rural Affairs, 1855-6-7*, Vol. 1. Albany: Luther Tucker and Son, 1858.

[24] Kenny, D. J., *Illustrated Cincinnati.* Cincinnati: Robert Clarke and Co., 1875.

[25] *King's Handbook of Boston*, 9th ed. Boston: Moses King Corporation, 1889.

[26] McCabe, James D., *Illustrated History of the Centennial Exhibition.* Philadelphia: Jones Brothers and Co., 1876.

[27] ————, *Our Country and Its Resources,* Philadelphia: Hubbard Bros., 1876.

[28] McQuill, Thursty, *The Connecticut by Daylight.* New York: American News Co., 1874.

[29] Mellen, Greenville, ed., *A Book of the United States.* New York: George Clinton Smith and Co., 1839.

[30] Moore, Joseph West, *Picturesque Washington.* Providence: J. A. and R. A. Reid, 1888.

[31] Nason, Elias, *A Gazeteer of the State of Massachusetts.* Boston: B. B. Russell, 1874.

[32] *Official Souvenir: Grand Encampment of Knights Templar.* Boston: 1895.

[33] Peck, Frederick M., and Earl, Henry H., *Fall River and Its Industries.* New York: Atlantic Publishing and Engraving, 1877.

[34] Petri and Pelsing, engraving after the painting by F. Guy.

[35] *Pictorial National Library.* Boston: William Simonds, 1849.

[36] Reed, S. B., *Cottage Houses for Village and Country Homes.* New York: Orange Judd Co., 1883.

[37] Seabury, Samuel, *Two Hundred and Seventy-five Years of East Hampton.* New York: Bartlett Orr Press, 1926.

[38] Sears, Robert, *Pictorial Description of the United States.* New York: Robert Sears, 1848.

[39] Shannon, Joseph, *Manual of the Corporation of the City of New York.* New York: E. Jones and Co., 1869.

[40] Simson, Matthew, *Cyclopedia of Methodism.* Philadelphia: Louis H. Everts, 1881.

[41] Stark, James H., *Stark's Antique Views of Ye Towne of Boston.* Boston: Morse-Purce Co., 1907.

[42] Studer, Jacob H., *Columbus, Ohio.* Columbus: Jacob H. Studer, 1873.

[43] Walker, A. H., *Atlas of Bergen County.* Reading: Reading Publishing House, 1876.

[44] Wheeler, Gervase, *Homes for the People, in Suburb and Country.* New York: George E. Woodward, 1867.

[45] Willis, William, *A Business Directory of the Subscribers to the New Map of Maine, with a Brief History of the State.* Portland: J. Chace, Jr. and Co., 1862.

[46] *The World We Live in.* New York: Hunt and Eaton, 1893.

Index

All references are to figure numbers.

A CATALOG OF SELECTED

DOVER BOOKS

IN ALL FIELDS OF INTEREST

A CATALOG OF SELECTED DOVER
BOOKS IN ALL FIELDS OF INTEREST

CONCERNING THE SPIRITUAL IN ART, Wassily Kandinsky. Pioneering work by father of abstract art. Thoughts on color theory, nature of art. Analysis of earlier masters. 12 illustrations. 80pp. of text. 5⅜ × 8½.   23411-8 Pa. $3.95

ANIMALS: 1,419 Copyright-Free Illustrations of Mammals, Birds, Fish, Insects, etc., Jim Harter (ed.). Clear wood engravings present, in extremely lifelike poses, over 1,000 species of animals. One of the most extensive pictorial sourcebooks of its kind. Captions. Index. 284pp. 9 × 12.   23766-4 Pa. $10.95

CELTIC ART: The Methods of Construction, George Bain. Simple geometric techniques for making Celtic interlacements, spirals, Kells-type initials, animals, humans, etc. Over 500 illustrations. 160pp. 9 × 12. (USO)   22923-8 Pa. $8.95

AN ATLAS OF ANATOMY FOR ARTISTS, Fritz Schider. Most thorough reference work on art anatomy in the world. Hundreds of illustrations, including selections from works by Vesalius, Leonardo, Goya, Ingres, Michelangelo, others. 593 illustrations. 192pp. 7⅛ × 10¼.   20241-0 Pa. $8.95

CELTIC HAND STROKE-BY-STROKE (Irish Half-Uncial from "The Book of Kells"): An Arthur Baker Calligraphy Manual, Arthur Baker. Complete guide to creating each letter of the alphabet in distinctive Celtic manner. Covers hand position, strokes, pens, inks, paper, more. Illustrated. 48pp. 8¼ × 11.
24336-2 Pa. $3.95

EASY ORIGAMI, John Montroll. Charming collection of 32 projects (hat, cup, pelican, piano, swan, many more) specially designed for the novice origami hobbyist. Clearly illustrated easy-to-follow instructions insure that even beginning papercrafters will achieve successful results. 48pp. 8¼ × 11.   27298-2 Pa. $2.95

THE COMPLETE BOOK OF BIRDHOUSE CONSTRUCTION FOR WOOD-WORKERS, Scott D. Campbell. Detailed instructions, illustrations, tables. Also data on bird habitat and instinct patterns. Bibliography. 3 tables. 63 illustrations in 15 figures. 48pp. 5¼ × 8½.   24407-5 Pa. $1.95

BLOOMINGDALE'S ILLUSTRATED 1886 CATALOG: Fashions, Dry Goods and Housewares, Bloomingdale Brothers. Famed merchants' extremely rare catalog depicting about 1,700 products: clothing, housewares, firearms, dry goods, jewelry, more. Invaluable for dating, identifying vintage items. Also, copyright-free graphics for artists, designers. Co-published with Henry Ford Museum & Greenfield Village. 160pp. 8¼ × 11.   25780-0 Pa. $8.95

HISTORIC COSTUME IN PICTURES, Braun & Schneider. Over 1,450 costumed figures in clearly detailed engravings—from dawn of civilization to end of 19th century. Captions. Many folk costumes. 256pp. 8⅜ × 11¾.   23150-X Pa. $10.95

STICKLEY CRAFTSMAN FURNITURE CATALOGS, Gustav Stickley and L. & J. G. Stickley. Beautiful, functional furniture in two authentic catalogs from 1910. 594 illustrations, including 277 photos, show settles, rockers, armchairs, reclining chairs, bookcases, desks, tables. 183pp. 6½ × 9¼. 23838-5 Pa. $8.95

AMERICAN LOCOMOTIVES IN HISTORIC PHOTOGRAPHS: 1858 to 1949, Ron Ziel (ed.). A rare collection of 126 meticulously detailed official photographs, called "builder portraits," of American locomotives that majestically chronicle the rise of steam locomotive power in America. Introduction. Detailed captions. xi + 129pp. 9 × 12. 27393-8 Pa. $12.95

AMERICA'S LIGHTHOUSES: An Illustrated History, Francis Ross Holland, Jr. Delightfully written, profusely illustrated fact-filled survey of over 200 American lighthouses since 1716. History, anecdotes, technological advances, more. 240pp. 8 × 10¾. 25576-X Pa. $10.95

TOWARDS A NEW ARCHITECTURE, Le Corbusier. Pioneering manifesto by founder of "International School." Technical and aesthetic theories, views of industry, economics, relation of form to function, "mass-production split" and much more. Profusely illustrated. 320pp. 6⅛ × 9¼. (USO) 25023-7 Pa. $8.95

HOW THE OTHER HALF LIVES, Jacob Riis. Famous journalistic record, exposing poverty and degradation of New York slums around 1900, by major social reformer. 100 striking and influential photographs. 233pp. 10 × 7⅞.
22012-5 Pa $10.95

FRUIT KEY AND TWIG KEY TO TREES AND SHRUBS, William M. Harlow. One of the handiest and most widely used identification aids. Fruit key covers 120 deciduous and evergreen species; twig key 160 deciduous species. Easily used. Over 300 photographs. 126pp. 5⅜ × 8½. 20511-8 Pa. $2.95

COMMON BIRD SONGS, Dr. Donald J. Borror. Songs of 60 most common U.S. birds: robins, sparrows, cardinals, bluejays, finches, more—arranged in order of increasing complexity. Up to 9 variations of songs of each species.
Cassette and manual 99911-4 $8.95

ORCHIDS AS HOUSE PLANTS, Rebecca Tyson Northen. Grow cattleyas and many other kinds of orchids—in a window, in a case, or under artificial light. 63 illustrations. 148pp. 5⅜ × 8½. 23261-1 Pa. $3.95

MONSTER MAZES, Dave Phillips. Masterful mazes at four levels of difficulty. Avoid deadly perils and evil creatures to find magical treasures. Solutions for all 32 exciting illustrated puzzles. 48pp. 8¼ × 11. 26005-4 Pa. $2.95

MOZART'S DON GIOVANNI (DOVER OPERA LIBRETTO SERIES), Wolfgang Amadeus Mozart. Introduced and translated by Ellen H. Bleiler. Standard Italian libretto, with complete English translation. Convenient and thoroughly portable—an ideal companion for reading along with a recording or the performance itself. Introduction. List of characters. Plot summary. 121pp. 5¼ × 8½.
24944-1 Pa. $2.95

TECHNICAL MANUAL AND DICTIONARY OF CLASSICAL BALLET, Gail Grant. Defines, explains, comments on steps, movements, poses and concepts. 15-page pictorial section. Basic book for student, viewer. 127pp. 5⅜ × 8½.
21843-0 Pa. $3.95

BRASS INSTRUMENTS: Their History and Development, Anthony Baines. Authoritative, updated survey of the evolution of trumpets, trombones, bugles, cornets, French horns, tubas and other brass wind instruments. Over 140 illustrations and 48 music examples. Corrected and updated by author. New preface. Bibliography. 320pp. 5⅜ × 8½.   27574-4 Pa. $9.95

HOLLYWOOD GLAMOR PORTRAITS, John Kobal (ed.). 145 photos from 1926–49. Harlow, Gable, Bogart, Bacall; 94 stars in all. Full background on photographers, technical aspects. 160pp. 8⅜ × 11¼.   23352-9 Pa. $9.95

MAX AND MORITZ, Wilhelm Busch. Great humor classic in both German and English. Also 10 other works: "Cat and Mouse," "Plisch and Plumm," etc. 216pp. 5⅜ × 8½.   20181-3 Pa. $5.95

THE RAVEN AND OTHER FAVORITE POEMS, Edgar Allan Poe. Over 40 of the author's most memorable poems: "The Bells," "Ulalume," "Israfel," "To Helen," "The Conqueror Worm," "Eldorado," "Annabel Lee," many more. Alphabetic lists of titles and first lines. 64pp. 5³⁄₁₆ × 8¼.   26685-0 Pa. $1.00

SEVEN SCIENCE FICTION NOVELS, H. G. Wells. The standard collection of the great novels. Complete, unabridged. First Men in the Moon, Island of Dr. Moreau, War of the Worlds, Food of the Gods, Invisible Man, Time Machine, In the Days of the Comet. Total of 1,015pp. 5⅜ × 8½. (USO)   20264-X Clothbd. $29.95

AMULETS AND SUPERSTITIONS, E. A. Wallis Budge. Comprehensive discourse on origin, powers of amulets in many ancient cultures: Arab, Persian, Babylonian, Assyrian, Egyptian, Gnostic, Hebrew, Phoenician, Syriac, etc. Covers cross, swastika, crucifix, seals, rings, stones, etc. 584pp. 5⅜ × 8½. 23573-4 Pa. $10.95

RUSSIAN STORIES/PYCCKNE PACCKA3bI: A Dual-Language Book, edited by Gleb Struve. Twelve tales by such masters as Chekhov, Tolstoy, Dostoevsky, Pushkin, others. Excellent word-for-word English translations on facing pages, plus teaching and study aids, Russian/English vocabulary, biographical/critical introductions, more. 416pp. 5⅜ × 8½.   26244-8 Pa. $7.95

PHILADELPHIA THEN AND NOW: 60 Sites Photographed in the Past and Present, Kenneth Finkel and Susan Oyama. Rare photographs of City Hall, Logan Square, Independence Hall, Betsy Ross House, other landmarks juxtaposed with contemporary views. Captures changing face of historic city. Introduction. Captions. 128pp. 8¼ × 11.   25790-8 Pa. $9.95

AIA ARCHITECTURAL GUIDE TO NASSAU AND SUFFOLK COUNTIES, LONG ISLAND, The American Institute of Architects, Long Island Chapter, and the Society for the Preservation of Long Island Antiquities. Comprehensive, well-researched and generously illustrated volume brings to life over three centuries of Long Island's great architectural heritage. More than 240 photographs with authoritative, extensively detailed captions. 176pp. 8¼ × 11.   26946-9 Pa. $14.95

NORTH AMERICAN INDIAN LIFE: Customs and Traditions of 23 Tribes, Elsie Clews Parsons (ed.). 27 fictionalized essays by noted anthropologists examine religion, customs, government, additional facets of life among the Winnebago, Crow, Zuni, Eskimo, other tribes. 480pp. 6⅛ × 9¼.   27377-6 Pa. $10.95

FRANK LLOYD WRIGHT'S HOLLYHOCK HOUSE, Donald Hoffmann. Lavishly illustrated, carefully documented study of one of Wright's most controversial residential designs. Over 120 photographs, floor plans, elevations, etc. Detailed perceptive text by noted Wright scholar. Index. 128pp. 9¼ × 10¾. 27133-1 Pa. $10.95

THE MALE AND FEMALE FIGURE IN MOTION: 60 Classic Photographic Sequences, Eadweard Muybridge. 60 true-action photographs of men and women walking, running, climbing, bending, turning, etc., reproduced from rare 19th-century masterpiece. vi + 121pp. 9 × 12. 24745-7 Pa. $10.95

1001 QUESTIONS ANSWERED ABOUT THE SEASHORE, N. J. Berrill and Jacquelyn Berrill. Queries answered about dolphins, sea snails, sponges, starfish, fishes, shore birds, many others. Covers appearance, breeding, growth, feeding, much more. 305pp. 5¼ × 8¼. 23366-9 Pa. $7.95

GUIDE TO OWL WATCHING IN NORTH AMERICA, Donald S. Heintzelman. Superb guide offers complete data and descriptions of 19 species: barn owl, screech owl, snowy owl, many more. Expert coverage of owl-watching equipment, conservation, migrations and invasions, etc. Guide to observing sites. 84 illustrations. xiii + 193pp. 5⅜ × 8½. 27344-X Pa. $7.95

MEDICINAL AND OTHER USES OF NORTH AMERICAN PLANTS: A Historical Survey with Special Reference to the Eastern Indian Tribes, Charlotte Erichsen-Brown. Chronological historical citations document 500 years of usage of plants, trees, shrubs native to eastern Canada, northeastern U.S. Also complete identifying information. 343 illustrations. 544pp. 6½ × 9¼. 25951-X Pa. $12.95

STORYBOOK MAZES, Dave Phillips. 23 stories and mazes on two-page spreads: Wizard of Oz, Treasure Island, Robin Hood, etc. Solutions. 64pp. 8¼ × 11. 23628-5 Pa. $2.95

NEGRO FOLK MUSIC, U.S.A., Harold Courlander. Noted folklorist's scholarly yet readable analysis of rich and varied musical tradition. Includes authentic versions of over 40 folk songs. Valuable bibliography and discography. xi + 324pp. 5⅜ × 8½. 27350-4 Pa. $7.95

MOVIE-STAR PORTRAITS OF THE FORTIES, John Kobal (ed.). 163 glamor, studio photos of 106 stars of the 1940s: Rita Hayworth, Ava Gardner, Marlon Brando, Clark Gable, many more. 176pp. 8⅜ × 11¼. 23546-7 Pa. $10.95

BENCHLEY LOST AND FOUND, Robert Benchley. Finest humor from early 30s, about pet peeves, child psychologists, post office and others. Mostly unavailable elsewhere. 73 illustrations by Peter Arno and others. 183pp. 5⅜ × 8½. 22410-4 Pa. $4.95

YEKL and THE IMPORTED BRIDEGROOM AND OTHER STORIES OF YIDDISH NEW YORK, Abraham Cahan. Film Hester Street based on Yekl (1896). Novel, other stories among first about Jewish immigrants on N.Y.'s East Side. 240pp. 5⅜ × 8½. 22427-9 Pa. $5.95

SELECTED POEMS, Walt Whitman. Generous sampling from *Leaves of Grass*. Twenty-four poems include "I Hear America Singing," "Song of the Open Road," "I Sing the Body Electric," "When Lilacs Last in the Dooryard Bloom'd," "O Captain! My Captain!"—all reprinted from an authoritative edition. Lists of titles and first lines. 128pp. 5³⁄₁₆ × 8¼. 26878-0 Pa. $1.00

THE BEST TALES OF HOFFMANN, E. T. A. Hoffmann. 10 of Hoffmann's most important stories: "Nutcracker and the King of Mice," "The Golden Flowerpot," etc. 458pp. 5⅜ × 8½. 21793-0 Pa. $8.95

FROM FETISH TO GOD IN ANCIENT EGYPT, E. A. Wallis Budge. Rich detailed survey of Egyptian conception of "God" and gods, magic, cult of animals, Osiris, more. Also, superb English translations of hymns and legends. 240 illustrations. 545pp. 5⅜ × 8½. 25803-3 Pa. $10.95

FRENCH STORIES/CONTES FRANÇAIS: A Dual-Language Book, Wallace Fowlie. Ten stories by French masters, Voltaire to Camus: "Micromegas" by Voltaire; "The Atheist's Mass" by Balzac; "Minuet" by de Maupassant; "The Guest" by Camus, six more. Excellent English translations on facing pages. Also French-English vocabulary list, exercises, more. 352pp. 5⅜ × 8½. 26443-2 Pa. $8.95

CHICAGO AT THE TURN OF THE CENTURY IN PHOTOGRAPHS: 122 Historic Views from the Collections of the Chicago Historical Society, Larry A. Viskochil. Rare large-format prints offer detailed views of City Hall, State Street, the Loop, Hull House, Union Station, many other landmarks, circa 1904–1913. Introduction. Captions. Maps. 144pp. 9⅜ × 12¼. 24656-6 Pa. $12.95

OLD BROOKLYN IN EARLY PHOTOGRAPHS, 1865–1929, William Lee Younger. Luna Park, Gravesend race track, construction of Grand Army Plaza, moving of Hotel Brighton, etc. 157 previously unpublished photographs. 165pp. 8⅞ × 11¾. 23587-4 Pa. $12.95

THE MYTHS OF THE NORTH AMERICAN INDIANS, Lewis Spence. Rich anthology of the myths and legends of the Algonquins, Iroquois, Pawnees and Sioux, prefaced by an extensive historical and ethnological commentary. 36 illustrations. 480pp. 5⅜ × 8½. 25967-6 Pa. $8.95

AN ENCYCLOPEDIA OF BATTLES: Accounts of Over 1,560 Battles from 1479 B.C. to the Present, David Eggenberger. Essential details of every major battle in recorded history from the first battle of Megiddo in 1479 B.C. to Grenada in 1984. List of Battle Maps. New Appendix covering the years 1967–1984. Index. 99 illustrations. 544pp. 6½ × 9¼. 24913-1 Pa. $14.95

SAILING ALONE AROUND THE WORLD, Captain Joshua Slocum. First man to sail around the world, alone, in small boat. One of great feats of seamanship told in delightful manner. 67 illustrations. 294pp. 5⅜ × 8½. 20326-3 Pa. $4.95

ANARCHISM AND OTHER ESSAYS, Emma Goldman. Powerful, penetrating, prophetic essays on direct action, role of minorities, prison reform, puritan hypocrisy, violence, etc. 271pp. 5⅜ × 8½. 22484-8 Pa. $5.95

MYTHS OF THE HINDUS AND BUDDHISTS, Ananda K. Coomaraswamy and Sister Nivedita. Great stories of the epics; deeds of Krishna, Shiva, taken from puranas, Vedas, folk tales; etc. 32 illustrations. 400pp. 5⅜ × 8½. 21759-0 Pa. $8.95

BEYOND PSYCHOLOGY, Otto Rank. Fear of death, desire of immortality, nature of sexuality, social organization, creativity, according to Rankian system. 291pp. 5⅜ × 8½. 20485-5 Pa. $7.95

A THEOLOGICO-POLITICAL TREATISE, Benedict Spinoza. Also contains unfinished Political Treatise. Great classic on religious liberty, theory of government on common consent. R. Elwes translation. Total of 421pp. 5⅜ × 8½. 20249-6 Pa. $7.95

EARLY NINETEENTH-CENTURY CRAFTS AND TRADES, Peter Stockham (ed.). Extremely rare 1807 volume describes to youngsters the crafts and trades of the day: brickmaker, weaver, dressmaker, bookbinder, ropemaker, saddler, many more. Quaint prose, charming illustrations for each craft. 20 black-and-white line illustrations. 192pp. 4⅝ × 6. 27293-1 Pa. $4.95

VICTORIAN FASHIONS AND COSTUMES FROM HARPER'S BAZAR, 1867–1898, Stella Blum (ed.). Day costumes, evening wear, sports clothes, shoes, hats, other accessories in over 1,000 detailed engravings. 320pp. 9⅜ × 12¼.
22990-4 Pa. $12.95

GUSTAV STICKLEY, THE CRAFTSMAN, Mary Ann Smith. Superb study surveys broad scope of Stickley's achievement, especially in architecture. Design philosophy, rise and fall of the Craftsman empire, descriptions and floor plans for many Craftsman houses, more. 86 black-and-white halftones. 31 line illustrations. Introduction. 208pp. 6½ × 9¼. 27210-9 Pa. $9.95

THE LONG ISLAND RAIL ROAD IN EARLY PHOTOGRAPHS, Ron Ziel. Over 220 rare photos, informative text document origin (1844) and development of rail service on Long Island. Vintage views of early trains, locomotives, stations, passengers, crews, much more. Captions. 8⅞ × 11¾. 26301-0 Pa. $13.95

THE BOOK OF OLD SHIPS: From Egyptian Galleys to Clipper Ships, Henry B. Culver. Superb, authoritative history of sailing vessels, with 80 magnificent line illustrations. Galley, bark, caravel, longship, whaler, many more. Detailed, informative text on each vessel by noted naval historian. Introduction. 256pp. 5⅜ × 8½. 27332-6 Pa. $6.95

TEN BOOKS ON ARCHITECTURE, Vitruvius. The most important book ever written on architecture. Early Roman aesthetics, technology, classical orders, site selection, all other aspects. Morgan translation. 331pp. 5⅜ × 8½. 20645-9 Pa. $8.95

THE HUMAN FIGURE IN MOTION, Eadweard Muybridge. More than 4,500 stopped-action photos, in action series, showing undraped men, women, children jumping, lying down, throwing, sitting, wrestling, carrying, etc. 390pp. 7⅞ × 10⅝. 20204-6 Clothbd. $24.95

TREES OF THE EASTERN AND CENTRAL UNITED STATES AND CANADA, William M. Harlow. Best one-volume guide to 140 trees. Full descriptions, woodlore, range, etc. Over 600 illustrations. Handy size. 288pp. 4½ × 6⅜.
20395-6 Pa. $4.95

SONGS OF WESTERN BIRDS, Dr. Donald J. Borror. Complete song and call repertoire of 60 western species, including flycatchers, juncoes, cactus wrens, many more—includes fully illustrated booklet. Cassette and manual 99913-0 $8.95

GROWING AND USING HERBS AND SPICES, Milo Miloradovich. Versatile handbook provides all the information needed for cultivation and use of all the herbs and spices available in North America. 4 illustrations. Index. Glossary. 236pp. 5⅜ × 8½. 25058-X Pa. $5.95

BIG BOOK OF MAZES AND LABYRINTHS, Walter Shepherd. 50 mazes and labyrinths in all—classical, solid, ripple, and more—in one great volume. Perfect inexpensive puzzler for clever youngsters. Full solutions. 112pp. 8⅛ × 11.
22951-3 Pa. $3.95

PIANO TUNING, J. Cree Fischer. Clearest, best book for beginner, amateur. Simple repairs, raising dropped notes, tuning by easy method of flattened fifths. No previous skills needed. 4 illustrations. 201pp. 5⅜ × 8½.   23267-0 Pa. $4.95

A SOURCE BOOK IN THEATRICAL HISTORY, A. M. Nagler. Contemporary observers on acting, directing, make-up, costuming, stage props, machinery, scene design, from Ancient Greece to Chekhov. 611pp. 5⅜ × 8½.   20515-0 Pa. $10.95

THE COMPLETE NONSENSE OF EDWARD LEAR, Edward Lear. All nonsense limericks, zany alphabets, Owl and Pussycat, songs, nonsense botany, etc., illustrated by Lear. Total of 320pp. 5⅜ × 8½. (USO)   20167-8 Pa. $5.95

VICTORIAN PARLOUR POETRY: An Annotated Anthology, Michael R. Turner. 117 gems by Longfellow, Tennyson, Browning, many lesser-known poets. "The Village Blacksmith," "Curfew Must Not Ring Tonight," "Only a Baby Small," dozens more, often difficult to find elsewhere. Index of poets, titles, first lines. xxiii + 325pp. 5⅜ × 8¼.   27044-0 Pa. $7.95

DUBLINERS, James Joyce. Fifteen stories offer vivid, tightly focused observations of the lives of Dublin's poorer classes. At least one, "The Dead," is considered a masterpiece. Reprinted complete and unabridged from standard edition. 160pp. 5³⁄₁₆ × 8¼.   26870-5 Pa. $1.00

THE HAUNTED MONASTERY and THE CHINESE MAZE MURDERS, Robert van Gulik. Two full novels by van Gulik, set in 7th-century China, continue adventures of Judge Dee and his companions. An evil Taoist monastery, seemingly supernatural events; overgrown topiary maze hides strange crimes. 27 illustrations. 328pp. 5⅜ × 8½.   23502-5 Pa. $7.95

THE BOOK OF THE SACRED MAGIC OF ABRAMELIN THE MAGE, translated by S. MacGregor Mathers. Medieval manuscript of ceremonial magic. Basic document in Aleister Crowley, Golden Dawn groups. 268pp. 5⅜ × 8½.
23211-5 Pa. $7.95

NEW RUSSIAN-ENGLISH AND ENGLISH-RUSSIAN DICTIONARY, M. A. O'Brien. This is a remarkably handy Russian dictionary, containing a surprising amount of information, including over 70,000 entries. 366pp. 4½ × 6⅛.
20208-9 Pa. $8.95

HISTORIC HOMES OF THE AMERICAN PRESIDENTS, Second, Revised Edition, Irvin Haas. A traveler's guide to American Presidential homes, most open to the public, depicting and describing homes occupied by every American President from George Washington to George Bush. With visiting hours, admission charges, travel routes. 175 photographs. Index. 160pp. 8¼ × 11. 26751-2 Pa. $10.95

NEW YORK IN THE FORTIES, Andreas Feininger. 162 brilliant photographs by the well-known photographer, formerly with *Life* magazine. Commuters, shoppers, Times Square at night, much else from city at its peak. Captions by John von Hartz. 181pp. 9¼ × 10¾.   23585-8 Pa. $12.95

INDIAN SIGN LANGUAGE, William Tomkins. Over 525 signs developed by Sioux and other tribes. Written instructions and diagrams. Also 290 pictographs. 111pp. 6⅛ × 9¼.   22029-X Pa. $3.50

ANATOMY: A Complete Guide for Artists, Joseph Sheppard. A master of figure drawing shows artists how to render human anatomy convincingly. Over 460 illustrations. 224pp. 8⅜ × 11¼.   27279-6 Pa. $9.95

MEDIEVAL CALLIGRAPHY: Its History and Technique, Marc Drogin. Spirited history, comprehensive instruction manual covers 13 styles (ca. 4th century thru 15th). Excellent photographs; directions for duplicating medieval techniques with modern tools. 224pp. 8⅜ × 11¼.   26142-5 Pa. $11.95

DRIED FLOWERS: How to Prepare Them, Sarah Whitlock and Martha Rankin. Complete instructions on how to use silica gel, meal and borax, perlite aggregate, sand and borax, glycerine and water to create attractive permanent flower arrangements. 12 illustrations. 32pp. 5⅜ × 8½.   21802-3 Pa. $1.00

EASY-TO-MAKE BIRD FEEDERS FOR WOODWORKERS, Scott D. Campbell. Detailed, simple-to-use guide for designing, constructing, caring for and using feeders. Text, illustrations for 12 classic and contemporary designs. 96pp. 5⅜ × 8½.
25847-5 Pa. $2.95

OLD-TIME CRAFTS AND TRADES, Peter Stockham. An 1807 book created to teach children about crafts and trades open to them as future careers. It describes in detailed, nontechnical terms 24 different occupations, among them coachmaker, gardener, hairdresser, lacemaker, shoemaker, wheelwright, copper-plate printer, milliner, trunkmaker, merchant and brewer. Finely detailed engravings illustrate each occupation. 192pp. 4⅝ × 6.   27398-9 Pa. $4.95

THE HISTORY OF UNDERCLOTHES, C. Willett Cunnington and Phyllis Cunnington. Fascinating, well-documented survey covering six centuries of English undergarments, enhanced with over 100 illustrations: 12th-century laced-up bodice, footed long drawers (1795), 19th-century bustles, 19th-century corsets for men, Victorian "bust improvers," much more. 272pp. 5⅜ × 8¼.   27124-2 Pa. $9.95

ARTS AND CRAFTS FURNITURE: The Complete Brooks Catalog of 1912, Brooks Manufacturing Co. Photos and detailed descriptions of more than 150 now very collectible furniture designs from the Arts and Crafts movement depict davenports, settees, buffets, desks, tables, chairs, bedsteads, dressers and more, all built of solid, quarter-sawed oak. Invaluable for students and enthusiasts of antiques, Americana and the decorative arts. 80pp. 6½ × 9¼.   27471-3 Pa. $7.95

HOW WE INVENTED THE AIRPLANE: An Illustrated History, Orville Wright. Fascinating firsthand account covers early experiments, construction of planes and motors, first flights, much more. Introduction and commentary by Fred C. Kelly. 76 photographs. 96pp. 8¼ × 11.   25662-6 Pa. $7.95

THE ARTS OF THE SAILOR: Knotting, Splicing and Ropework, Hervey Garrett Smith. Indispensable shipboard reference covers tools, basic knots and useful hitches; handsewing and canvas work, more. Over 100 illustrations. Delightful reading for sea lovers. 256pp. 5⅜ × 8½.   26440-8 Pa. $6.95

FRANK LLOYD WRIGHT'S FALLINGWATER: The House and Its History, Second, Revised Edition, Donald Hoffmann. A total revision—both in text and illustrations—of the standard document on Fallingwater, the boldest, most personal architectural statement of Wright's mature years, updated with valuable new material from the recently opened Frank Lloyd Wright Archives. "Fascinating"—*The New York Times.* 116 illustrations. 128pp. 9¼ × 10¾.
27430-6 Pa. $10.95

THE WIT AND HUMOR OF OSCAR WILDE, Alvin Redman (ed.). More than 1,000 ripostes, paradoxes, wisecracks: Work is the curse of the drinking classes; I can resist everything except temptation; etc. 258pp. 5⅜ × 8½.   20602-5 Pa. $4.95

SHAKESPEARE LEXICON AND QUOTATION DICTIONARY, Alexander Schmidt. Full definitions, locations, shades of meaning in every word in plays and poems. More than 50,000 exact quotations. 1,485pp. 6½ × 9¼. 2-vol. set.
Vol. 1: 22726-X Pa. $15.95
Vol. 2: 22727-8 Pa. $15.95

SELECTED POEMS, Emily Dickinson. Over 100 best-known, best-loved poems by one of America's foremost poets, reprinted from authoritative early editions. No comparable edition at this price. Index of first lines. 64pp. 5³⁄₁₆ × 8¼.
26466-1 Pa. $1.00

CELEBRATED CASES OF JUDGE DEE (DEE GOONG AN), translated by Robert van Gulik. Authentic 18th-century Chinese detective novel; Dee and associates solve three interlocked cases. Led to van Gulik's own stories with same characters. Extensive introduction. 9 illustrations. 237pp. 5⅜ × 8½.
23337-5 Pa. $5.95

THE MALLEUS MALEFICARUM OF KRAMER AND SPRENGER, translated by Montague Summers. Full text of most important witchhunter's "bible," used by both Catholics and Protestants. 278pp. 6⅝ × 10.   22802-9 Pa. $10.95

SPANISH STORIES/CUENTOS ESPAÑOLES: A Dual-Language Book, Angel Flores (ed.). Unique format offers 13 great stories in Spanish by Cervantes, Borges, others. Faithful English translations on facing pages. 352pp. 5⅜ × 8½.
25399-6 Pa. $7.95

THE CHICAGO WORLD'S FAIR OF 1893: A Photographic Record, Stanley Appelbaum (ed.). 128 rare photos show 200 buildings, Beaux-Arts architecture, Midway, original Ferris Wheel, Edison's kinetoscope, more. Architectural emphasis; full text. 116pp. 8¼ × 11.   23990-X Pa. $9.95

OLD QUEENS, N.Y., IN EARLY PHOTOGRAPHS, Vincent F. Seyfried and William Asadorian. Over 160 rare photographs of Maspeth, Jamaica, Jackson Heights, and other areas. Vintage views of DeWitt Clinton mansion, 1939 World's Fair and more. Captions. 192pp. 8⅞ × 11.   26358-4 Pa. $12.95

CAPTURED BY THE INDIANS: 15 Firsthand Accounts, 1750–1870, Frederick Drimmer. Astounding true historical accounts of grisly torture, bloody conflicts, relentless pursuits, miraculous escapes and more, by people who lived to tell the tale. 384pp. 5⅜ × 8½.   24901-8 Pa. $7.95

THE WORLD'S GREAT SPEECHES, Lewis Copeland and Lawrence W. Lamm (eds.). Vast collection of 278 speeches of Greeks to 1970. Powerful and effective models; unique look at history. 842pp. 5⅜ × 8½.   20468-5 Pa. $12.95

THE BOOK OF THE SWORD, Sir Richard F. Burton. Great Victorian scholar/adventurer's eloquent, erudite history of the "queen of weapons"—from prehistory to early Roman Empire. Evolution and development of early swords, variations (sabre, broadsword, cutlass, scimitar, etc.), much more. 336pp. 6⅛ × 9¼. 25434-8 Pa. $8.95

THE INFLUENCE OF SEA POWER UPON HISTORY, 1660–1783, A. T. Mahan. Influential classic of naval history and tactics still used as text in war colleges. First paperback edition. 4 maps. 24 battle plans. 640pp. 5⅜ × 8½.
25509-3 Pa. $12.95

THE STORY OF THE TITANIC AS TOLD BY ITS SURVIVORS, Jack Winocour (ed.). What it was really like. Panic, despair, shocking inefficiency, and a little heroism. More thrilling than any fictional account. 26 illustrations. 320pp. 5⅜ × 8½.
20610-6 Pa. $7.95

FAIRY AND FOLK TALES OF THE IRISH PEASANTRY, William Butler Yeats (ed.). Treasury of 64 tales from the twilight world of Celtic myth and legend: "The Soul Cages," "The Kildare Pooka," "King O'Toole and his Goose," many more. Introduction and Notes by W. B. Yeats. 352pp. 5⅜ × 8½.
26941-8 Pa. $7.95

BUDDHIST MAHAYANA TEXTS, E. B. Cowell and Others (eds.). Superb, accurate translations of basic documents in Mahayana Buddhism, highly important in history of religions. The Buddha-karita of Asvaghosha, Larger Sukhavativyuha, more. 448pp. 5⅜ × 8½. ,
25552-2 Pa. $9.95

ONE TWO THREE . . . INFINITY: Facts and Speculations of Science, George Gamow. Great physicist's fascinating, readable overview of contemporary science: number theory, relativity, fourth dimension, entropy, genes, atomic structure, much more. 128 illustrations. Index. 352pp. 5⅜ × 8½.
25664-2 Pa. $7.95

ENGINEERING IN HISTORY, Richard Shelton Kirby, et al. Broad, nontechnical survey of history's major technological advances: birth of Greek science, industrial revolution, electricity and applied science, 20th-century automation, much more. 181 illustrations. ". . . excellent . . ."—Isis. Bibliography. vii + 530pp. 5⅜ × 8¼.
26412-2 Pa. $13.95